CO
SECRETARIAL PRACTICE IN INDIA: A PRACTICAL APPROACH

MW01241862

-AVTAR SINGH

Dedicated to
My late mother
Sardarni Gurdev Kaur
and
late father
Sardar Ram Singh

Copyright @2021 Avtar Singh

Preface

The book 'Corporate Secretarial Practice in India: a practical approach', is an attempt by the author to simplify the subject for readers. The objective is to make it is easy for those who want to know more about the Secretarial Practice and also for those who want to adopt it as a profession.

The implementation of the Companies Act 2013 has increased substantially the value of Secretarial Practice and consequently the demand for Company Secretaries has also gone up. It therefore becomes necessary to give a direction to prospective company secretaries in a simple and lucid manner. The book has explained the provisions of the new companies act and the secretarial standards. The websites of Ministry of Company Affairs and Institute of Company Secretaries of India have been referred in writing the book.

A book of this magnitude cannot be possible without drawing references from various sources books, journals, government publications, websites etc. The author is deeply indebted to all authors whose works have left an influence on the present work.

It is my bounden duty to thank the almighty but for whose beneficence no work would be possible. I have always felt his invisible presence and accept that but for his grace this work would not have seen the light of the day. Last but not the least I thank my better half Mrs Sarabjeet Kaur and sons CA Prabhjot Singh and Amandeep Singh who helped us tremendously in various ways. They bore my rather indifferent attention towards them without complaints.

I sincerely hope the readers would find the work useful and help me by making free, frank and honest suggestions.

- **Dr. Avtar Singh**

Contents

Preface

CHAPTER 1

COMPANY SECRETARY

A secretary is defined by the Oxford Dictionary as "one whose office is to write for another, especially one who is employed to conduct correspondence, to keep records and to transact various other businesses for another person or for a society, corporation or public body".

Therefore the Secretary of Company is one of the principal officers of the company with the requisite qualifications to undertake secretarial work and management of the affairs of the company as per the provisions of the Act and instructions laid down by the Board of Directors. The Board, however, cannot alter the duties of the secretary as they are determined by the law

Definition of Company Secretary

The definitions of company secretary as per the Companies Act, 2013 and the Company Secretaries Act, 1980 are as follows:

According to section 2(24) of the Companies Act, 2013, "Company Secretary or secretary means a company secretary as defined in clause (c) of sub-section (1) of section 2 of the Company Secretaries Act, 1980 who is appointed by a company to perform the functions of a company secretary under this Act".

According to section 2 (1) (c) of the Company Secretaries Act, 1980, "a company secretary is a person who is a member of the Institute of Company Secretaries of India".

Appointment of Company Secretary

This section contains the provisions of the statutes relating to appointment of Company Secretary. This may be divided into two parts

1. Appointment of First Secretary or Pro Tem Secretary.
2. Appointment of whole time Secretary
3. Pro Tem Secretary

Usually the first secretary who helps in fulfilling the various formalities is appointed by the promoters of a company. He/ She is known as pro tem secretary.

The pro tem secretary appointed by the promoters may or may not be appointed as regular secretary by the Board. Even when the name of the first secretary is mentioned in the Articles, it does not bind the company to appoint that very person as its secretary, because Articles bind the company to its members only and it does not constitute an agreement between the company and the outsiders. Therefore, if the *pro tem* secretary is not appointed as the first secretary by the Board after incorporation of the company, he/she cannot sue the company. However, he/she should be given a proper notice; otherwise, he/she can sue the company for the damages.

The pro tem secretary must immediately after the incorporation secure his/ her position by getting a resolution passed by the Board at the first Board meeting. This resolution appointing a person as the secretary of the company should contain the terms and conditions of his appointment including the remuneration.

APPOINTMENT OF WHOLE TIME COMPANY SECRETARY

In this section the various provisions of the statutes which concerns the appointment of Company Secretary have been explained.

Mandatory Appointment of Whole Time Company Secretary

Section 203 of the Companies Act 2013 read along with Companies (Appointment and Remuneration of Managerial Personnel) Rules, 2014, provides that every listed company and every other public company having a paid-up share capital of rupees ten crores or more shall appoint the Company Secretary who is in whole-time employment. Such a provision was not applicable for private companies or public companies that had paid up share capital of a less than rupees ten crores. As a result this provision was very much in debate as it limited the role of Company Secretary in private companies or in public companies that had paid up capital of less than rupees ten crores. Therefore, on 9th June 2014 Ministry of Corporate Affairs inserted Rule 8A vide Notification No. G.S.R. 390(E) which reads as follows:

"A company other than a company covered under rule 8 which has a paid up share capital of five crore rupees or more shall have a whole-time company secretary". Now the following classes of companies must appoint a company secretary.

- Any listed company.
- Unlisted public company having paid up share capital of rupees five crores or more.
- Any private company having a paid-up share capital of rupees five crores or more.

Process to Appoint a Company Secretary

Call Board Meeting: As per Section 203(2) a resolution should be passed by the Board of Directors for Appointment of Company Secretary. Board Resolution should contain the following

- Terms and Conditions of Appointment.
- Remuneration.
- Membership No.

Consent to act as Company Secretary:

The appointed company secretary shall give a written consent to act as Company Secretary of the company.

Consent to act As Company Key Managerial Person (KMP):

The appointed company secretary shall give a written consent to act as a key managerial person of the company.

Filing of documents: the following documents should be filed by the company to the Registrar of Companies.

- MGT-14: As per provision of Section 179 (3) Rule 8(2) the companyis required to file MGT- 14 within 30 days of passing of Board Resolution with Consent Letter and copy of Board Resolution.

- MR-1: As per Rule 3 of Chapter XIII acompany is required to file MR-1 at the time of appointment of Key Managerial Person within 60 days of passing of Board Resolution, with copy of Board Resolution and Consent Letter.

- DIR- 12: As per Section 170 (2) a company is required to file form DIR-12 for appointment of Director or KMP within 30 days of passing of Board resolution along with Consent Letter, Appointment Letter, Self attested Copy of PAN card and copy of Board Resolution.

1. A company secretary can be removed or dismissed like any other employees of the organization. Since he is appointed by Board, the Board of directors of a company has absolute discretion to remove a company secretary or to terminate his services at any time for any reason or without any reason. However, principles of natural justice like show cause notice, hearing, reasoned order etc. must be followed.

2. Qualifications of a Company Secretary

In order to be appointed a Secretary of a company a person should possess one of the following qualifications.

- Member of the Institute of Company Secretaries of India constituted under the Company Secretaries Act, 1980 (56 of 1980).

- Member of the Institute of Company Secretaries of India constituted under the Company Secretaries Act, 1980 (56 of 1980).

- Pass in the Intermediate examination conducted either by the Institute of Company Secretaries of India constituted under the Company Secretaries Act, 1980 (No. 56 of 1980), or by the earlier Institute of Company Secretaries of India incorporated on 4th October, 1968, under the Companies Act, 1956 (1 of 1956), and licensed under section 25 of that Act.

- Post-graduate degree in commerce or corporate secretaryship granted by any university in India.Degree in law granted by any university.

- Member of the Institute of Chartered Accountants of India constituted under the Chartered Accountants Act, 1949 (38 of 1949).

- Member of the Institute of Cost and Works Accountants of India constituted under the Cost and Works Accountants Act, 1959 (23 of 1959).

- Post-graduate degree or diploma in management sciences, granted by any university, or the Institutes of Management, Ahmedabad, Calcutta, Bangalore or Lucknow.

- Post-graduate diploma in company secretary ship granted by the Institute of Commercial Practice under the Delhi Administration or Diploma in Corporate Laws and Management granted by the Indian Law Institute, New Delhi.

- Post-graduate diploma in company law and secretarial practice granted by the University of Udaipur; or

- Member of the Association of Secretaries and Managers, Calcutta, registered under the West Bengal Registration of Societies Act, 1961 (XXVI of 1961) : Provided that where the paid-up share capital of such company is increased to rupees twenty-five lakhs or more, the company shall, within a period of one year from the date of such increase, comply with the provisions of sub-rules (1) and (2) of rule 2.

Manner of Appointment of whole-time company secretary [(Sec. 203(2)]

A whole time company secretary should be appointed by means of a resolution passed by the Board of directors. Such a resolution should contain the terms and conditions of the appointment of the whole time company secretary including his/her remuneration.

Ceiling on number of offices held [(Section 203 (3)]

A whole time company secretary shall not hold office in more than one company except in its subsidiary company at the same time.

In case a whole time company secretary is holding office in more than one company at the time of commencement of this Act, he/she shall choose one company in which he wishes to hold office as a whole time company secretary within a period of 6 months from the commencement of this Act. However a whole time company secretary may be appointed as a director of any company only with the prior permission of the Board of Directors of the company in which he/she is holding office as a Company Secretary.

Vacation of Office [(Section 203 (4)]

If the office of the whole time company secretary falls vacant due to any reason, then such a vacancy shall be filled up by the Board of directors within a period of 6 months from the date of such vacancy.

Penal Provisions

If a company contravenes the provisions of this section:

- The company shall be punishable with fine which shall not be less than one lakh rupees but which may extend to five lakh rupees.
- Every director and key managerial personnel of the company who is in default shall be punishable with fine which may extend to fifty thousand rupees.
- Where the contravention is a continuing one, with a further fine which may extend to one thousand rupees for every day after the first during which the contravention continues.

DUTIES OF COMPANY SECRETARIES

The duties of company secretary can be classified into general duties and statutory duties.

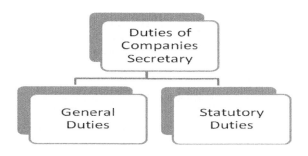

1. General Duties:

- Should be present in all meetings of the company and of the directors and has to prepare proper minutes of the proceedings of the meetings.

- Issues all necessary notices to members and others under the direction of the Board.

- Corresponds with shareholders in regard to further issues of shares and calls, making of transfers and forfeitures is in-charge of the books of the company.

- Performs administrative functions and is responsible for filing all necessary returns with the Registrar of Companies.

2. Statutory Duties:

The Rule 10 of the Companies (Appointment and Remuneration of Managerial Personnel) Rules, 2014 holds that the company secretary shall discharge the following duties:

- To provide to information to the directors of the company, collectively and individually, such guidance as they may require, with regard to their duties, responsibilities and powers;

- To facilitate the convening of meetings and attend Board, committee and general meetings and maintain the minutes of these meetings; To obtain approvals from the Board, general meeting, the government and such other authorities as required under the provisions of the Act;

- To represent before various regulators, and other authorities under the Act in connection with discharge of various duties under the Act.

- To assist the Board in the conduct of the affairs of the company.

- To assist and advise the Board in ensuring good corporate governance and in complying with the corporate governance requirements and best practices.

- To discharge such other duties as have been specified under the Act or rules.

- Such other duties as may be assigned by the Board from time to time.

Liabilities of Company Secretary

The liabilities of company secretary can be grouped under two broad heads:

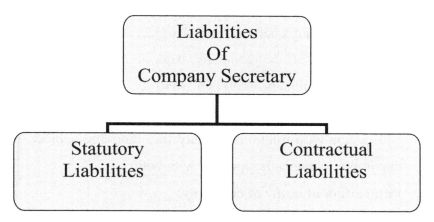

Statutory Liabilities

- **Filing returns as regards allotment:**
  Default in filing returns as regards allotment with in prescribed time he shall be punishable with fine which may extend up to one thousand rupees for every day during which default continues or one lakh rupees, Whichever is less.

- **Preparation of share/debenture certificates:**
  In case of default, the company secretary shall be punishable with fine which shall not be less than ten thousand rupees subject to maximum one lakh rupees.

- **Register of Members/ Debentureholders**:
  Failure will make company secretary punishable with fine which shall not be less than fifty thousand rupees but which

may be extended upto three lakh rupees and where the failure is continuing one, with a further fine which may be extended upto one thousand rupees every day.

- **Filing of particulars regarding charges**:

  If a default is made in the filing with the Registrar the particulars of any charge of any charge created by company, every officer of the company who is in default which includes a company secretary shall be punishable with imprisonment for a term which may extend to six months or with a fine with minimum twenty five thousand subject to maximum to one lakh rupees or with both.

- **Publication of name of company**:

  If the default is made in getting the name and address of the registered office of the company painted or affixed or printed outside every office or place of business or printed on all its business letters, bill heads etc. If Company Secretary is in default shall be liable to a penalty of one thousand rupees every day during the default continues to maximum one lakh rupees.

- **Filing annual returns**:

  If Company Secretary fails to file annual return as per requirement of act; he shall be punishable with a fine not less than fifty thousand which may be extended upto five lakh rupees.

- **Holding annual general meeting:**

  Default in holding annual general meeting in accordance with company acts shall make him liable to a fine which may extend to one lakh rupees and in case of a continuing default with fine which may be extended to five thousand rupees for every day during which default continues.

- **Circulation of member's resolutions:**

  If a default is made in circulating members resolution of which they have given notice to the company, he shall be punishable with fine which may extend to Rs 25,000.

- **Registering certain resolutions and agreements:**

  This default is punishable with a fine which shall not less than one lakh rupees which may be extended up to five lakh rupees.

Recording the minutes of the meeting:

- If a default is made in recording the minutes of all proceedings of every general meeting and meetings of board, a fine of Rs 5,000 may be levied on every officer in default which includes company secretary.

- Maintaining minute books or allowing inspection or furnishing copies of minutes to members.

- If default is made in furnishing a copy of minutes with in seven working days after the date of request by any member or if inspection is not allowed, he shall be liable for fine of Rs 5,000 for each such refusal or default, as the case may be

- **Notice of Board's meeting**:

   Board meeting shall be called by giving at least seven days' notice in writing to every director at his registered address with company by hand or by post or by electronic means. Failure on this make every officer of company whose duty is to give notice shall be liable to penalty of twenty five thousand only.

- **Register of directors and key managerial personnel and their shareholding**:

   Company Secretary in default shall be punishable with a fine which shall not less than one lakh rupees which may be extended up to five lakh rupees.

- **Register of inter-corporate loans and investment**:

   For this default Company Secretary in default shall be punishable with imprisonment for term which may extend to two years and with fine which shall not less than twenty five thousand rupees which may be extended up to one lakh rupees.

In addition to above mentioned liabilities under Company Act, Company Secretary is responsible under various other provisions of Income tax Act, Indian Stamps Act, Employees state Insurance Act, Factories Act, Minimum wages Act, payment of wages act, Industrial disputes act. The company secretary is also principal officer responsible to fulfill the duties cast upon him under the foreign exchange Management act (FEMA).

Contractual Liabilities

A company Secretary enters into service contract with the company and accordingly he has several contractual liabilities which arise out of his service agreement which are as follows:

- Company secretary derives his powers from board; therefore he should carry out the orders given to him.

- He should never allow his personal interest to clash with interest of company.

- He shall be liable to account for the secret profit made by him by virtue of his position.

- He shall be personally liable if he acts beyond his authority,

- He shall be liable for any loss or damage caused to company by willful misconduct or negligence in the discharge of his duties.

- He shall be liable for any fraud or wrong committed in the course of his employment.

- However, if the secretary performs his duties honestly, he shall not be held responsible. The Secretary shall also not be liable for any fraud by his assistants unless he is party to such fraud.

Role of company secretary under Companies Act 2013

The Companies Act has strengthened the role of company secretaries. Some of the key areas that have directly impact the role of company secretaries in employment or in practice due to this Act are as follows:

1.   **Introduction of secretarial audit**:

Secretarial Audit is the process to check whether the company is adhering to the legal and procedural requirements and a process to monitor the company's compliance with the requirements of the stated laws. The objective behind the introduction of secretarial audit is to improve corporate governance and compliance.

According to Section 204 of the Companies Act 2013, it is the duty of the Company Secretary in practice to perform secretarial audit of every listed company and any such other class of prescribed companies. The Central Government has prescribed the other class of prescribed companies as-

- o Every public company with a paid-up share capital of Rs. 50 Crore or more.

- o Every public company with a turnover of Rs. 250 Crore or more.

2.   **Secretarial standards**:

The objective behind the formulation of secretarial standards is to integrate, harmonize and standardization of diverse secretarial practices. The Companies Act, 2013 under Section 118 has made the compliance of Secretarial Standards compulsory on meeting of the Board of Directors and on general meetings.

3.   **Annual return**:

Annual return is a comprehensive document contains information regarding share capital, directors, shareholders, changes in directorships etc about the company. Under the old Companies Act of 1956 the annual return of the listed companies are required to be signed by the company secretary in practice. The new Companies Act, 2013 under Section 92 has widened this requirement by providing that annual returns of companies having such paid up capital and turnover to be signed and certified by the company secretaries in practice.

4.   **Appointment of whole-time key managerial personnel**:

Under Section 203 of the new Companies Act, 2013, the companies has to compulsorily appoint the whole time Key Managerial Personnel in respect of certain class of companies as prescribed by the Central Government to ensure good corporate

17

governance and regulation. The company shall have the following whole-time Key Managerial Personnel (KMP):

- Managing Director, or Chief Executive Officer or manager and in their absence, a whole-time director.

- Company Secretary.

- Chief Financial Officer.

So this made the appointment of whole-time Company Secretary mandatory for better efficiency.

3. **Functions of company secretary:**

According to Section 205 of the Companies Act, 2013 the Company Secretary shall discharge following functions and duties, this is the first time that the duties of the company secretary have been specified in the company law:

- To report to the Board about the compliance with the provisions of this Act.

- To ensure that the company complies with the applicable secretarial standards.

- To provide to the directors of the company the guidance they require in discharging their duties, responsibilities and powers.

- To facilitate the convening of meetings and attend Board, committee and general meetings and maintain the minutes of these meetings.

- To obtain approvals from the Board, general meeting, the government and such other authorities as required under the provisions of the Act.

- To assist the Board in the conduct of the affairs of the company.

- To assist and advise the Board in ensuring good corporate governance and in complying with the corporate governance requirements and best practices.

Procedure for Removal/Resignation of a Company Secretary

- A Company Secretary can be removed in accordance with the terms of appointment and the Board can record the same.

- Convene a Board meeting after giving notice to all the directors of the company as per section 173, place the matter of removal/resignation of the Company Secretary and pass a resolution to the effect.

- File Form DIR-12 in electronic mode within thirty days with the Registrar of Companies together with requisite filing fees. Evidence of Cessation (for example Resignation Letter) is an optional attachment.

- Inform the stock exchange where the company is listed.

- Make entries in the Register maintained for recording the particulars of Company Secretaries under section 170.

- Issue a general public notice, if it is so warranted, according to size and nature of the company.

- The resulting vacancy shall be filled up by the Board at a meeting of the Board within a period of six months from the date of such vacancy.

Removal of Company Secretary in Practice:

A Company Secretary in practice can be removed *suo-motu* by the engaging Company or if found guilty of professional misconduct in the manner specified in Schedule I of the Company Secretaries Act, 1980 by the Institute and his name is removed from the Register of Members.

A Board resolution to this effect is to be passed at the Board meeting of the Company. In case the company is listed company, then notify such removal to the stock exchange immediately after Board meeting.

COMPANY SECRETARY IN PRACTICE

According to Section 2(25) of the Companies Act, 2013 "company secretary in practice" means a company secretary who is deemed to be in practice under sub-section (2) of Section 2 of the Company Secretaries Act, 1980.

Section 2(2) of the Company Secretaries Act, 1980 provides that a member of the Institute shall be deemed "to be in practice" when, individually or in partnership with one or more members of the Institute in practice or in partnership with members of such other recognized professions as may be prescribed, he, in consideration of remuneration received or to be received,-

The Companies Act, 2013 has considerably enhanced the role and responsibilities of company secretaries both in employment and in practice. While the Companies Act, 2013 has opened up a significant area of practice for Company Secretaries, it casts immense responsibility on Company Secretaries, and poses a great challenge to justify fully, the faith and confidence reposed in them.

A practicing company secretary should pay particular attention to the following are

      1.   **Incorporation of company [Section 7]:** Section 7 lays down the procedure for incorporation of a company. A company was incorporated by submitting memorandum and articles duly signed along with a declaration in prescribed form to the effect that the requirements of the Act in respect of registration have been complied with. Section 7 (1) of the Act provides that there shall be filed with the Registrar within whose jurisdiction the registered office of a company is proposed to be situated, the following documents and information for registration, namely:-

(a) the memorandum and articles of the company duly signed by all the subscribers to the memorandum in such manner as may be prescribed. (b) a declaration in the prescribed form by an advocate, a chartered accountant, cost accountant or company secretary in practice, who is engaged in the formation of the company, and by a person named in the articles as a director, manager or secretary of the company, that all the requirements of this Act and the rules made thereunder in respect of registration and matters precedent or incidental thereto have been complied with.Therefore, company secretary in practice along with other professionals has vast scope at the time of incorporation of a company.

2. Signing of Annual Return (Section 92): Every company shall prepare a return (hereinafter referred to as the annual return) in the prescribed form containing the particulars as they stood on the close of the financial year signed by a director and the company secretary, or Where there is no company secretary, by a company secretary in practice, Provided that in relation to One Person Company and small company, the annual return shall be signed by the company secretary, or where there is no company secretary, by the director of the company.

The annual return, filed by a listed company or, by a company having such paid-up capital and turnover as may be prescribed, shall be certified by a company secretary in practice in the prescribed form, stating that the annual return discloses the facts correctly and adequately and that the company has complied with all the provisions of this Act.

As per Companies (Management and Administration) Rules, 2014, such prescribed class means a listed company or a company having paid-up share capital of ten crore rupees or more or turnover of fifty crore rupees or more.Section 92(6) of the Act provides that if a company secretary in practice certifies the annual return otherwise than in conformity with the requirements of this section or the rules made thereunder, he shall be punishable with fine which shall not be less than fifty thousand rupees but which may extend to five lakh rupees. Thus, concerned company secretary in practice shall remain vigilant while certifying the annual return of the companies. He should disclose all facts correctly, adequately and in compliance with all provisions of the Companies Act, 2013.

4. Voting through electronic means:

Every listed company or a company having not less than one thousand shareholders, provide to its members facility to exercise their right to vote at general meetings by electronic means.During the e-voting period, shareholders holding shares either in physical form or in dematerialized form, as on the record date, may cast their vote electronically.

- Once the vote on a resolution is cast by the shareholder, he shall not be allowed to change it subsequently.

- The Board of directors to appoint one scrutinizer, who may be chartered Accountant in practice, Cost Accountant in practice, or Company Secretary in practice or an advocate, but not in employment of the company and is a person of repute who, in the opinion of the Board can scrutinize the e-voting process in a fair and transparent manner.

- The scrutinizer to maintain a register either manually or electronically to record the assent or dissent, received and other details as provided under the rules.

- Manner in which the Chairman of meeting shall get the poll process scrutinized and report thereon is provided under the rules. The company secretary in practice has a very important role as a scrutinizer in case of voting through electronic means.

4.   **Report on annual general meeting [Section1 21]:** Every listed public company shall prepare a report on each annual general meeting including the confirmation to the effect that the meeting was convened, held and conducted as per the provisions of the Act and the rules made thereunder. A copy of this report shall be filed with the Registrar. Company Secretary is authorized to sign the report on every Annual General Meeting along with two

directors one of whom shall be the Managing Director if there is one.

5.   **Secretarial Audit for Bigger Companies [Section 204]:** Every listed company and a company belonging to other class of companies as may be prescribed shall annex with its Board's report made in terms of sub-section (3) of section 134, a secretarial audit report, given by a company secretary in practice, in such form as may be prescribed. The Board of Directors, in their report made in terms of sub-section (3) of section 134, shall explain in full any qualification or observation or other remarks made by the company secretary in practice in his report.

This exclusive provision of secretarial audit report shall help compliance on the part of listed companies to a better level. It shall curb fraudulent manipulations by listed companies and related group companies. The Act has made it obligatory to comment the Board of Directors on the adverse remarks of a Practicing Company Secretary in his secretarial audit report. This will certainly help in enhancing the usefulness of secretarial auditing. Secretarial audit would provide great scope to practicing company secretaries as well.

6.   **Appointment as Administrator [Section 259]:** Company Secretaries along with other professionals have been recognized for being appointed as Interim/ Company Administrator from the panel to be maintained by the Central Government or any

institute or agency authorized by the Central Government, in respect of rehabilitation of revival and sick companies.

7. **Company Liquidators [Section 275]:** Section 275 provides for appointment of official liquidator or liquidators for the purpose of winding up of a company from a panel of professionals maintained by the Central Government as the company liquidator. Such professional must be having at least ten years of experience in company matters or such other qualifications. Company Secretaries have been recognized to be appointed as Provisional Liquidator or the Company Liquidator, from a panel to be maintained by the Central Government.

8. **Professional assistance to Company Liquidator (Section 291):** The Company Liquidator may, with the sanction of the Tribunal, appoint one or more professionals including Company Secretaries on such terms and conditions, as may be necessary, to assist him in the performance of his duties and functions under the Act.

9. **Qualifications of President and Members of Tribunal (Section 409)**: The constitution of National Company Law Appellate Tribunal (NCLT) shall widen the scope of services of practicing company secretaries. A Company Secretary in practice is eligible to become a Technical Member of National Company law Tribunal, if he is practicing for at least fifteen years.

10. **Right to legal representation (Section 432):** Section 432 of the Act enables a party to any proceeding to appear in person or to authorize professionals including company secretaries to present the case before the Tribunal or the Appellate Tribunal.

11. **Merger and amalgamation of Companies [Section 232]:** Filing of statement every year until completion of scheme [Section 232(7)]: Every company in relation to which the order is made shall, until the completion of the scheme, file a statement in such form and within such time as may be prescribed with the Registrar every year duly certified by a chartered accountant or a cost accountant or a company secretary in practice indicating whether the scheme is being complied with in accordance with the orders of the Tribunal or not.

12. **Certification under Listing Agreement**: As per clause 47(c) of the equity listing agreement, company has to ensure that the Registrar and/orShare Transfer Agent (RTA) and/or officers from the in-house Share Transfer department, as the casemay be, obtain a certificate from a practising company secretary within one month of the end of each half of the financial year, certifying that all certificates have been issued within fifteen days of the date of lodgement for transfer, sub-division, consolidation, renewal, exchange or endorsement of calls/allotment monies. A copy of the said certificate should be made available to

the concerned stock exchange within 24 hours of the receipt of the certificate by the company.

Further clause 49 (XI) of the equity listing agreement relating to Corporate Governance lays down that the company shall obtain a certificate from either the auditors or practicing company secretaries regarding compliance of conditions of corporate governance as stipulated in that clause and annex the certificate with the directors' report, which is sent annually to all the shareholders of the company. The same certificate shall also be sent to the Stock Exchanges along with the annual report filed by the company.

Under section 6(1) of the Company Secretaries Act, 1980, no member of the Institute shall be entitled to practice whether in India or elsewhere unless he has obtained from the Council of the Institute a certificate of practice.

CHAPTER 2

Company Meetings

A company is an artificial person which exists in contemplation of law. As a legal entity it has an existence separate from its members. Thus it can act in its own name, enter into contracts, can own property in its own name, and can sue others and be sued in its own name. Thus, it has all the powers available to a natural person but it cannot act on its own. It expresses its will through resolutions passed at meetings which should necessarily fall within the purview of law.

All the decisions of the company are moved during the course of meetings. Such decisions are called resolutions. A company is owned by members who are called shareholders. The shareholders are numerous and geographically scattered. It is not possible for them to meet often. Therefore they elect a Board of directors which runs the affairs of the company. The powers of the company are divided between the board and the shareholders. According to Section 179 of the Companies Act 2013 the board of directors of a company shall be entitled to exercise all such powers, and to do all such acts and things, as the company shall be entitled to do. But for the purpose of exercising their powers or for taking decisions the shareholders or directors have to come together in a manner provided by the law, proceed according to the law in order to take decisions as per law. Thus the decisions taken by the shareholders or directors can be valid only if taken in a meeting which is valid as per the provisions of the companies act.

The role of the company secretary in convening and conducting the meeting is of utmost importance. The company secretary should be aware of the various requirements of the company act relating to meetings. He should ensure that meetings are held as per the provisions of law and cannot be challenged later on.

Statutory Meeting

According to Section 156 of the Companies Act 1956, Every Company limited by shares and every company limited by guarantee and having a share capital shall:

(i)   Within a period of not less than one month and

(ii)   Not more than six months from the date at which the company is entitled to commence business, hold a general meeting of the members of the company. This kind of meeting is known as Statutory Meeting.

Such a meeting is held on once during the life time of a company.

The following kinds of companies are not required to hold a statutory meeting

(i)   A private company.

(ii)   A public company not having share capital.

(iii)   A public company limited by guarantee and not having share capital.

(iv)   An unlimited company.

(v)   A government company.

Notice of statutory meeting

A notice for statutory meeting along with the statutory report must be given at least 21 clear days before the meeting. The notice should clarify that the meeting is a statutory meeting.

Notice to whom

The notice of the meeting should be given to

(i)   Every member of the company.

(ii)   Legal representative of a deceased member.

(iii)   Official receiver/assignee.

(iv)   Auditor of the company.

(v)   Public trustee in case shares are held in trust.

Statutory Report

It is necessary for the directors to send a report called Statutory Report to every member at least 21 days before the meeting.

Statutory Meeting under the Companies Act 2013

Under the new Companies Act 2013 which has become effective from 1st April, 2014, the provision relating to statutory meeting does not exist. Therefore it is no longer necessary for a company to hold any such meeting.

Kinds of meetings under the Companies Act 2013

The Companies Act, 2013 passed by the Parliament, received the Presidential assent on 29th August, 2013. The Act consolidates and amends the law relating to companies. The Companies Act, 2013 has been notified in the Official Gazette on 30th August, 2013. Some of the provisions of the Act have been implemented by a notification published on 12th September, 2013. The Act has come into effect since 1st April, 2014.

Meetings of Shareholders/General Meetings	Meetings of Directors and Committees	Other Meetings
• Annual General Meeting • Extra ordinary General Meeting • Class Meetings	• Meetings of Board of Directors • Audit Committee • Nomination Committee • Remuneration Committee • Stakeholders Relationship Committee	• Meetings of Debeture holders • Meetings of Creditors otherwise than in winding up. • Meetings of creditors and contributories in winding up. • Court Convened Meetings.

According to the Companies Act 2013, the various classes of meetings may be classified as follows:

Requisites of a valid General Meeting

Every meeting of the company should be in conformity with the Companies Act and the Articles of association. If the meeting fails to meet the requirements it would become invalid. A company meeting should satisfy the following requisites:

1. Proper Authority
2. Proper Notice
3. Business/Agenda
4. Proper Place, Time and Date
5. Quorum
6. Chairman
7. Proxy
8. Voting
9. Resolution
10. Minutes

1. Proper Authority

For any general meeting to be valid it is necessary that it is called by authorised persons or bodies who have been granted powers under the Act to do so. The following are entitled to convene a general meeting:

(a) Board of Directors,

(b) Members,

(c) National Company Law Board Tribunal.

Board of Directors: The power to call a general meeting (an annual general meeting as well as extra ordinary general meeting) vests with the board of directors, by common law. Section 100 of the Companies Act 2013 confers on the Board express powers to call an EGM. Thus generally the Articles of Association empower the Board to call a general meeting but if the Articles are silent the common law accords such powers on the Board. The new companies act has given the board, powers to call an extra ordinary general meeting.

➤ An individual director cannot call a general meeting, similarly the company secretary is not empowered to give a notice for calling a general meeting. But a company secretary can do so, if he is allowed to do so by the Board of Directors through a notice.

➤ In case the meeting of the Board of directors itself is unlawful e.g. where rightful directors are prevented from attending the directors' meeting, the decision taken by the Board at such meeting to call the general meeting, shall also be unlawful.

➤ Where, however, the meeting at which the directors decide to call a general meeting is not properly constituted (e.g. there is some defect in the appointment or qualification of the directors), and the Board acts bona fide, a general meeting called in pursuance of a resolution passed at such directors' meeting, is not necessarily invalid.

Members: Members who fulfil requirements of Section 100 can requisition an extra ordinary general meeting EGM. If the Board fails to call an extra ordinary general meeting within the time stipulated under this section, the eligible members can themselves call such a meeting. The eligibility of members and the procedure for holding an EGM under such circumstances has been elaborated in the next chapter. The members cannot call an Annual General Meeting.

National Company Law Tribunal: The National Company Law Tribunal can also call a general meeting as per the provisions of Section 97 and 98 of the Companies Act 2013. The details of such a meeting have given in the next chapter.

2. Notice (Section 101 of Companies Act 2013)

The Companies Act provides that a proper notice of the meeting should be given to the members and certain other persons well in advice so that they can prepare themselves.

Persons entitled to receive notice: Notice of every general meeting should be given to the following persons:

(i)   Every Director,

(ii)   Every Member,

(iii)   Legal representative of the deceased member,

(iv)   Official assignee of an insolvent member and

(v)   Auditor/s.

Length of Notice: Every member of the company is entitled to receive the notice at least 21 clear days before the meeting. According to Rule 35(6) of the Companies (Incorporation) Rules, 2014, where a notice of General Meeting is sent by post it shall be deemed to be served at the expiry of 48 hours after the letter containing the notice is posted. It has been further specified that part of the day on which the notice is deemed to be served on the member cannot be added to the part of the day up to the time of the General Meeting so as to make one day. Each of the 21 days must be complete days. In calculating 21 days, the date of receipt of notice and the date of the meeting should be excluded.

Articles may provide for a notice period longer than 21 days, but certainly not shorter than 21 days.

Example: A Ltd. gave a notice of its intention to hold its annual general meeting on 6th September, 2014. The notice was posted on 14th August, 2014 to members. Is the notice valid?

On the basis of the facts and provisions of the Companies Act 2013 contained in Section 101.

The notice will be considered to have been served on 17th August (after expiration of 48 Hours of despatch, 14th August, 2014 is to be excluded). There are a clear 19 days before 6th September (Since the day of AGM has to be excluded).Thus it can be concluded that the meeting is not valid. However the shortfall of two days can be condoned if 95% of the members entitled to vote give their consent to condone.

Shorter Notice: A general meeting may be called at a shorter notice, if, consent for a shorter notice is given by at least 95% of the members eligible to vote at a general meeting. Such consent may be obtained in writing or through electronic mode.

Service of Notice: The notice should be given in writing or by electronic mode, in the prescribed manner. Company may serve notice on the members either personally or by prepaid post or by advertisement in the newspaper. It must be properly addressed. Service of notice' by advertisement shall be deemed to be complete the day when the advertisement appears in the newspaper on both resident and non-resident members.

Contents of the notice: The notice must contain the following particulars:

(i)   It should specify the place, day, date and hour of the meeting and the meeting to be valid must be held at the place and time specified.

(ii)   It should also specify the business (Agenda) to be conducted at the meeting.

(iii)   The notice should also mention whether the meeting is AGM or EGM or a class meeting.

Effect of omission to give notice: Deliberate omission to give notice to a single member may invalidate the meeting. However, an accidental omission to give notice to or non-receipt of it, by a member will not invalidate the meeting.

Notice through electronic mode: 'Electronic mode' means any communication sent by a company through its authorised and secure computer programme which is capable of producing confirmation and keeping record of such communication at the last electronic mail address provided by the member. A company can give notice through electronic mode provided it is readable and the company gives complete Uniform Resource Locator (URL) of the website and full details of how to access the document or information.

Notice through e-mail: A company can send notice through email as a text message or as an attachment or by providing an electronic link or URL for accessing such website. The e-mail should be sent to the person entitled to receive the mail at the e-mail id as per records of the company or as provided by the depository. The company's obligation will be satisfied when it transmits the e-mail.

3. Business to be transacted at the meeting.

The notice of the general meetings should contain the agenda or the proposed business to be transacted. The business of the meeting can be classified into two categories:

(a) Ordinary Business and

(b) Special Business.

Ordinary Business: According to Section 102(2)(a), at the AGM, following business shall be treated as ordinary business

1.   Consideration and adoption of Financial Statements, Auditor's Report and Board of Directors' Report.

2.   Declaration of dividend.

3.   Retirement of directors and appointment of directors in the place of those retiring.

4.   Retirement of Auditors and appointment of auditors in place of those retiring.

At any other General Meeting no business shall be treated as ordinary business.

Special Business: At an AGM all business other than provided under Section 102(2)(a) shall be treated as special business. At any other General Meeting all business shall be deemed to be special business. The full text of the resolution must be given in the notice for transacting every item of special business. Explanatory statement must be annexed to the notice for transacting every item of special business.

Effect of non-disclosure: If, as a result of non-disclosure or insufficient disclosure in the explanatory statement, any benefit accrues to a promoter, director, manager or other key managerial personnel or their relatives, such person shall hold such benefit in trust for the company, and shall compensate the company to the extent of benefit derived by them.

Effective Date: Any notice of General Meeting issued on or after 12th September, 2013 shall have to comply with the provisions of Section 102 of the Companies Act 2013 (Ministry of Corporate Affairs Circular No. 15/2013).

5. Place, Date and Time of meeting

As per Section 96 (2), every annual general meeting shall be called during business hours, that is, between 9 a.m. and 6 p.m. on any day that is not aNational Holiday and shall be held either at the registered office of the company or at some other place within the city, town or village in which the registered office of the company is situated. As per draft Secretarial Standard on General Meetings (SS-2), general meeting(including EGM) shall be called during business hours i.e. between 9 a.m. and 6 p.m.and on a day that is not a National Holiday. A meeting called by the requisitionists shall be convened only on a working day.

Annual General Meetings shall be held either at the registered office of the company or at some other place within the city, town or village in which the registered office of the company is situated whereas other general meetings may be held at any place within India. As per explanation to Rule 17(2) of Companies (Management and Administration) Rules, 2014. A meeting called by the requisitionists shall be held either at the registered office of the company or at some other place within the city,town or village in which the registered office of the company is situated.

It has been further provided that the Central Government may exempt any company from the provisions of this sub-section subject to such conditions as it may impose.

National Holiday

Explanation to section 96 (2) provides that "National Holiday" means and includes a day declared as National Holiday by the Central Government.

As per draft Secretarial Standard-2, "National Holiday" includes Republic Day i.e.26th January, Independence Day i.e. 15th August, Gandhi Jayanti i.e. 2nd October and such other day as may be declared as National Holiday by the Central Government.The word 'National Holiday' used in Section 96 (2) of the Companies Act 2013 comes in place of the word 'Public Holiday' which was used in Section 166 (2) of the Companies Act 1956. The implication of this change is that a company can now hold a general meeting on any public holiday which is not a national holiday.

5. Quorum (Section 103 of the Companies Act 2013)

Minimum number of members required to constitute a valid meeting and to transact business therein is called 'quorum'. No meeting can be valid without quorum. Any resolution passed at a meeting without quorum shall be invalid.

Quorum for meetings is fixed by the Articles of Association of the company. But according to the Companies Act 2013, the minimum number of members required to attend a meeting are as follows. However the articles may fix a higher number than the below mentioned figures.

In case of Public Companies:

S.No.	Number of members as on the date of meeting	Quorum
1	Not more than 1000	5 members personally present
2	More than 1000 but not more than 5000	15 members personally present
3	More than 5000 members	30 members personally present

(b)   In case of Private Companies: 2 members personally present shall constitute quorum. However the articles may fix a higher number.

Legal effect of lack of quorum. If the requisite number of members is not present within half an hour from the appointed time for holding the General Meeting, the following will be the legal consequences.

(a)   An Extra ordinary meeting called by requisitionists u/s 100 – The meeting shall stand cancelled.

(b)   In case of any other meeting (AGM, EGM called by Board etc.)

(i)   The meeting shall adjourn to such day, time and place as may be determined by the Board.

(ii)   If the Board has not determined the day, time and place, the meeting shall adjourn to same day, time and place in the next week.

(iii)   At least 3 days' notice of adjourned meeting shall be given to the members either individually or by publishing an advertisement in 2 newspapers (one in English and one in vernacular language).

(iv)   If at an adjourned meeting also, a quorum is not present within half an hour from the time appointed for holding the meeting, the members present shall be the quorum.

When should the quorum be present during the meeting?

According to Secretarial standards on General meetings, the quorum should be present throughout the General Meeting. Thus, the quorum should be present not only at the time of commencement but also at the time of conduct of business. It need not be present throughout or at the time of taking the vote on any resolution. Thus, once a meeting is organised and all the parties have participated, no person or faction, by withdrawing capriciously and for the sole purpose of breaking the quorum can render the subsequent proceedings invalid.

Other issues relating to Quorum

➤ Members should be personally present at a Meeting to constitute the Quorum.

➤ Proxies shall be excluded for determining the Quorum.

➤ A duly authorised representative of a body corporate or the representative of the President of India or the Governor of a State is deemed to be a member personally present and enjoys all the rights of a member present in person.

➤ One person can be an authorised representative of more than one body corporate. In such a case, he is treated as more than one Member present in person for the purpose of Quorum. However, to constitute a Meeting, at least two individuals shall be present in person. Thus, in case of a public company having not more than 1000 members with a Quorum requirement of five Members, an authorised representative of five bodies corporate cannot form a Quorum by himself but can do so if at least one more Member is personally present.

➤ Members who have voted by Remote e-voting have the right to attend the General Meeting and accordingly their presence shall be, counted for the purpose of Quorum.

- A Member who is not entitled to vote on any particular item of business being a related party, if present, shall be counted for the purpose of Quorum.

- The stipulation regarding the presence of a Quorum does not apply with respect to items of business transacted through postal ballot.

- Preference Shareholders cannot be treated as members for the purpose of quorum since they can vote only on matters which affect their rights.

Can a single Member Constitute a Valid Meeting?

Ordinarily, a single member present cannot form a quorum, as a single member cannot constitute a meeting. This is because meeting prima facie means coming together of two or more than two persons. The Companies Act also uses the expression "members" which shows that more than one member is expected to be present.

Case: Sharp vs Dawes:

A meeting of a company was called to make a call. Out of several shareholders only one turned up. He had the proxies of other shareholders. He himself took the chair and passed a resolution making the call. He also proposed and passed a vote of thanks. It was held that the 'call' made was invalid since there was no meeting. The term meeting prima facie means the coming together of more than one person.

However, under certain exceptional situations one person can constitute a meeting

1.   When the Central Government calls or directs the calling of an annual general meeting.

2.   When the National Company Law Board Tribunal orders a meeting of a company (other than the annual general meeting).

3.   When a class of members or creditors consists of one person, that member alone can constitute the meeting of that class and can pass a resolution by signing it.

4.   When the Articles have allowed the Board of Directors to delegate some of their functions to a committee, which may consist of one person only.

Example: The articles of association of a company stipulate that 7 members shall constitute quorum. At an extra ordinary general meeting held the following persons were present to consider issue of sweat shares. Is the meeting valid?

(a) Four proxies for shareholders.

(b) One person representing Government of India.

(c) Two preference shareholders.

(d) One person representing two companies.

On the basis of the above facts and reference to the relevant provisions of Companies Act the following issues emerge

The four proxies cannot be considered members for the purpose of quorum because the law states that members should be personally present.

The representative of Government of India will be counted for the purpose.

The preference shareholders cannot be counted because the purpose of the meeting does not affect their rights.

One person representing two bodies corporate would be counted as two persons.

Thus only three persons are present, the meeting will not be valid because the articles stipulate the presence of 7 members.

6. Chairman (Section 104 of Companies Act, 2013)

A general meeting of the company is to be presided over by a chairman who regulates and supervises the proper conduct of the business at a meeting. He decides all incidental questions arising in the course of the proceedings of the meeting. Chairman should act bonafide and in the best interest of the company as a whole.

1.   Unless the articles of the company otherwise provide, the members personally present at the meeting shall elect one of themselves to be the Chairman thereof on a show of hands.

2.   If a poll is demanded on the election of the Chairman, it shall be taken forthwith in accordance with the provisions of this Act and the Chairman elected on a show of hands under sub-section (*1*) shall continue to be the Chairman of the meeting until some other person is elected as Chairman as a result of the poll, and such other person shall be the Chairman for the rest of the meeting.

Powers of a Chairman:

1.   The chairman has prima facie authority to decide all questions which arise at a meeting and which require decision at the time.

2.   The entry in the minute's book is evidence of the decisions taken at the meeting.

3.   The chairman has a right to decide priority amongst speakers, to demand poll, to exercise casting vote, to expel an unruly member and he may, with the support of the majority, apply closure to a discussion after it has been reasonably debated.

4.   He can adjourn a meeting when it is impossible, by reason of disorder or other like causes, to conduct the meeting and complete business.

Casting Vote:

Articles of Association may give an additional or second vote to the chairman of the company, over and above his right to vote as an ordinary member. In the case of a tie, i.e. equality of votes, chairman may use the casting vote to decide the matter in one way or the other.

Duties of a Chairman:

The chairman must take care to see that proper discipline is maintained at the meeting, that the proceedings are conducted in a proper manner, that proper opportunity is given to the members to express their views, that the voting is fair, and that the proceedings of the meeting are properly and correctly recorded in the minutes book.

The chairman should act bona fide according to his best ability and judgment and without any prejudices. He should see that the meeting is duly convened and properly held.

7. Proxy (Section 105 of Companies Act)

The term 'proxy' has two meanings:

(a)   A personal representative of the member at a meeting i.e. the person authorised to act or vote for another at a meeting of the company, and

(b)   The instrument by which a person is appointed to act for another at a meeting of the company, since a representative can be appointed only in writing.

The following are the provisions of the Companies Act regarding appointment and rights of proxy:

Members' right to appoint proxy.

Law entitles every member of a company to appoint a person as his proxy to attend and vote at company meeting instead of himself. However, a member of a company having no share capital does not have this right unless its articles provide otherwise.

Restrictions on appointment of Proxy

- ➢ The Central Government may prescribe a class or classes of companies whose members shall not be entitled to appoint another person as a proxy.

- ➢ A person can act as proxy on behalf of members:

    - o Not exceeding 50 and

    - o Holding in the aggregate not more than 10% of the total share capital of the company carrying voting rights.

- ➢ A member holding more than 10% of the total share capital of the company carrying voting rights may appoint a single person as proxy, provided that such person shall not act as proxy for any other person or shareholder.

Notice and disclosure regarding proxy

Every notice of the company regarding meeting should prominently contain a statement that a member entitled to attend and vote is authorised to appoint a proxy to attend and vote on his behalf. It should also be mentioned that the proxy need not be a member of the company.

Proxy to be deposited within 48 hours before the time of the meeting.

The instrument appointing a proxy must be deposited with the company within 48 hours before the meeting.

Legal requirements of proxy form

Proxy must be appointed by an instrument in writing, duly stamped and signed by the member of the company. A blank but stamped proxy is valid and may be completed by the person authorised to do so. Form no MGT-11 has been prescribed for the appointment of proxy.

Disabilities of a proxy

➢ A proxy has no right to speak at the meeting.

➢ A proxy cannot vote on a show of hands.

- A proxy does not have right to inspect proxy forms or minutes of meeting.

- A proxy is not counted for the purpose of quorum.

Rights of proxy

- A proxy has a right to attend the meeting.

- He has a right to vote in case of poll.

- A proxy if eligible under section 109, has a right to demand a poll.

Inspection

Any member can inspect the proxies deposited with the company. Inspection can be made by giving a notice of 3 days. Such inspection can be made during business hours commencing from 24 hours before the meeting and upto the conclusion of the meeting.

Revocation of Proxy

If the member himself attends the meeting after appointing a proxy, the appointment of proxy automatically stands cancelled. If the proxy exercises his right to vote it cannot be cancelled. Death of the shareholder appointing a proxy will, in the absence of provisions in the Articles revoke the authority of the proxy.

Can a body corporate appoint a proxy?

According to the Companies Act a body corporate can be a member or creditor of another company. The company can appoint a representative who will wield all powers of a regular member including being counted as a member for the purpose of quorum. The representative so appointed can appoint a proxy to attend and vote at the meeting in his place.

8. Voting

The decisions at the meetings are taken by way of passing resolutions. Every proposed resolution is discussed by the members of the company. Members have a right to move amendments to the proposed resolutions provided the amendments are relevant to the proposed resolution.

After a proposed resolution has been discussed it is put to vote. Every member has a right to vote on such resolutions. Shareholders may exercise their voting rights in their best interests with complete freedom.

Persons entitled to vote

Equity Shareholders. Every member of a company limited by shares and holding equity shares is entitled to vote in respect of every resolution placed before the company. The voting rights of members is in proportion to his paid up capital in the company.

Preference Shareholders. Preference shareholders are entitled to vote on resolutions which directly affect them.

Holders of share warrants. The holders of share warrants can vote only if the Articles of Association of the company so provide.

Joint holders. In cases where shares are held in joint names by two or more shareholders, the senior most among them will be entitled to vote. For the purpose of determination of seniority the order in which the name stands in the register of members shall be taken.

Insolvent. An insolvent member can exercise his right to vote if his name appears on the register of members.

Representatives of corporations. According to the Companies Act a body corporate can be a member or creditor of another company. The company can appoint a representative who will wield all powers of a regular member including being counted as a member for the purpose of quorum. The representative so appointed can appoint a proxy to attend and vote at the meeting in his place.

Representative of the President or Governor. The President of India or the governor of a state may appoint a representative to attend and vote on his behalf in meetings of companies in which he is a member. Such a representative shall be deemed to be a member of the company and shall be counted as a member for the purpose of quorum.

Manner of voting in General Meeting (Section 107 and 109 of Companies Act 2013)

Voting by show of hands (Section 107). Every resolution at a general meeting shall be decided by show of hands unless a poll is demanded under section 109 of the Companies Act, 2013 or where voting is carried electronically under section 108 of the Companies Act 2013. On a show of hands each member has one vote and the proxy is not entitled to vote. A declaration of the result of a resolution by the chairman and an entry in the minutes book shall be a conclusive proof that requisite number of votes has been cast in favour of the motion.

Voting by poll (Section 109). Poll is a method of voting in which votes are cast by a member in person or by proxy in proportion to the number of shares held by him.

Suo Motu action of chairman. The Chairman has a right to order a poll to be aken on any resolution either of his own motion or when it is validly demanded by one or more member/s. The chairman can order a poll before a resolution is put to vote on a show of hands or on the declaration of the result of voting by a show of hands.

Demand for poll. The chairman is required to order a poll in the following circumstances:

In case of a company having Share Capital:
Where demand is made by any member(s) present in person or proxy holding
$1/10^{th}$ of the total voting power, or

Paid up share capital of not less than Rs 5,00,000 or such higher amount as may be prescribed.

In case of any other company:

Any member/s present in person or proxy having $1/10^{th}$ voting power.

Time of ordering poll.

A poll may be ordered by the chairman before the declaration of the result of the voting on any resolution or on declaration of result. A poll cannot be demanded after the declaration of result and after the chairman has taken up any other item from the agenda for consideration.

Withdrawal of demand for poll.

A demand for poll may be withdrawn by the person/s who made such demand at any time before the result of the poll is declared.

Time of conduct of poll.

(a)   The poll shall be taken forthwith in case of adjournment of meeting or appointment of chairman.

(b)   The poll shall be taken at such time as may be directed by the Chairman but within 48 hours of demand for poll.

Powers of Chairman. The Chairman of the meeting shall have the powers to determine the manner in which the poll will be conducted. The Chairman shall appoint any number of scrutineers as he thinks is necessary for the conduct of the polls. The scrutineers shall scrutinise the poll process and votes given on the poll and report to the chairman.

Result of the poll. The result of the poll shall be deemed to be the decision of the meeting on the resolution on which the poll was taken.

Use votes differently. A member or proxy need not use all his votes or cast them in the same way. He may cast different votes for different resolutions..

Voting by electronic mode. Where a process of recording votes by the members using a computer based machine is known as voting by electronic mode. Under this electronic ballot is displayed and votes are recorded and the number of votes polled in favour or against is registered and counted in an electronic registry. According to section 108 of the Companies Act 2013, any company may opt for voting through electronic means. The central government may prescribe certain companies for compulsory electronic voting in general meetings.

9. Resolutions (Section 114 and 115 of the Companies Act 2013)

The decisions of members taken in a validly constituted meeting are called resolutions. Following are the various kinds of resolutions.

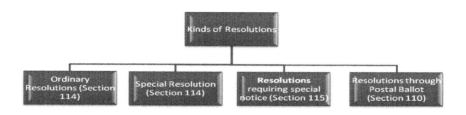

Ordinary Resolution. A resolution passed in a general meeting which is passed by a simple majority of eligible members and present during the meeting. To be a valid resolution the notice of 21 days required of a general meeting should have been given. The votes cast in favour of the resolution are required to exceed the votes cast against the resolution. Votes may be cast by way of show of hands, by poll, electronically, or by postal ballot. The votes may be cast by members present in person or proxies (where proxies are allowed). The votes cast shall include the casting vote of the chairman if any.

Special Resolution. A resolution will be a special resolution if

> ➢ The notice of General Meeting has been duly given. (21 days' notice has been given)

➢ The intention to propose the resolution as a special resolution has been duly specified in the notice of General Meeting or other intimation given to the members.

➢ The votes cast in favour of the resolution are required to be not less than 3 times the votes cast against the resolution.

➢ The articles of association may provide that certain types of business shall be approved by a special resolution. The Act also provides that in certain cases special resolution should be passed.

➢ A copy of every special resolution (together with explanatory statement) should be filed with the Registrar within 30 days of passing of such resolution (section 117 of Companies Act, 2013)

Resolution requiring special notice. Any provision contained in the Act may provide that a special notice shall be required to move a resolution at a General Meeting. Similarly any provision contained in the articles of a company may provide that special notice shall be required to move a resolution at a general meeting.

Legal requirements for special notice.

(a) The notice of intention to move a resolution requiring special notice shall be given to the company by such number of members holding not less than 1% of total voting power or holding shares on which such aggregate sum not exceeding ` 5 lakhs as may be prescribed, has been paid up.

(b)   Such notice should be given to the company not earlier than 3 months before the date of General Meeting but at least 14 days before the General Meeting (excluding the day on which such notice is given and the day of the General Meeting).

(c)   The notice should be signed by the eligible member/s as per point (a) above.

Communication of notice. On receipt of special notice the company shall notify the members in the following manner.

(a)   The company shall give notice of intention to move the resolution to all its members at least 7 days before the general meeting (excluding the day on which such notice is given and the day of the General Meeting).

(b)   The notice should be given in the same manner in which the notice of general meeting is given.

(c)   If it is not practicable to give the notice as specified above the notice should be published in an English and a Vernacular newspaper at least 7 days before the General Meeting (excluding the day on which such notice is given and the day of the General Meeting).

(d)   Such notice should also be placed on the website of the company if it has any such website.

Matters requiring special notice as per provisions of the Act. According to the Companies Act the following matters require special notice.

(a)   A resolution for appointing a person, other than the retiring auditor, as an auditor at the AGM. {Section 140(4)}.

(b)   A resolution for expressly providing that the retiring auditor shall not be reappointed at the AGM.

(c)   A resolution for removing a director before the expiry of his term of office {Section 169(2)}.

(d)   A resolution for appointing a director (in place of a director removed before the expiry of his period of office) at the meeting at which the director is removed {Section 169(2)}.

Passing of resolutions through Postal Ballot (Section 110 of the Companies Act 2013). According to Section 2(65), 'Postal Ballot' means voting by post or through any electronic mode. Every company is required to transact such items of business by postal ballot as the central government may by notification, declare to be transacted only by postal ballot. However any company may use postal ballot for transacting any item of business, other than ordinary business and any business in respect of which directors or auditors have a right to be heard at the meeting as an option where not mandatory.

Postal Ballot is mandatory for the following business.

- Alteration of object clause of Memorandum of Association.

- Alteration of articles for insertion or removal of provisions defining a private   company.

- Change in place of registered office outside the local limits of any city town or village.

- Change in the objects for which a company has raised money form public through prospectus and still has any unutilised amount out of the money so raised u/s 13(8).

- Issue of shares with differential rights as to voting or dividend or otherwise.

- Variation in the rights attached to a class of shares or debentures or other securities.

- Buy back of own shares by the company.

- Election of a small shareholders' director u/s 151 of the companies act 2013.

- Sale of the whole or substantially the whole of the undertaking u/s 180 (1) (a) of the Companies Act 2013.

- Giving loans, or extending guarantees or providing security in excess of the limits specified u/s 186 (3) of the Companies Act, 2013.

One person companies or all such companies which have a maximum of 200 members are not required to transact any business through postal ballot.

10. Minutes of General Meeting (Section 118 of Companies Act 2013)

It is necessary to record the proceedings of the meeting in order to keep a record for future reference. Such a record is known as 'Minutes'.

Legal requirement. According to Section 118 every company is required to prepare, and keep duly signed minutes of every general meeting, meeting of any class of shareholders, meeting of any class of creditors, meeting of board of directors, meeting of any committee and every resolution passed by postal ballot.

Manner of preparation and signatures. Minutes should contain a summary of the proceedings of the Meeting, recorded fairly, correctly, completely and in unambiguous terms, and should be written in third person and past tense. The minutes should be maintained in the books kept for that purpose. The pages of the minutes book should be consecutively numbered. Each page of the minutes book should be initialled or signed and the last page of the record of proceedings of the meeting shall be dated and signed. The minutes should be signed in the following manner:

- Minutes of Board and Committee meetings – the chairman of the same meeting or the chairman of the next meeting

- Meeting of General Meeting – The chairman of same meeting or in the event of the death or inability of that chairman by a director duly authorised by the board for this purpose.

- Resolutions passed by ballot – The chairman of the board or if there is no chairman in the event of death or inability of the chairman of the board by a director duly authorised by the board for the purpose.

Time limit. The minutes shall be prepared and signed within 30 days of the conclusion of the meeting or passing of the resolution by postal ballot.

Contents. The minutes should contain a summary of the proceedings. With reference to the Board meetings, the minutes should contain:

- the names of the directors present and

- where any resolution is passed at the meeting, the names of the directors dissenting from the resolution and the names of the directors not concurring with the resolution.

Chairman's Discretion. The chairman has absolute discretion to include or exclude any matter in the minutes if he is of the opinion that it is defamatory of any person, irrelevant, immaterial or detrimental to the interests of the company.

Evidence. As per Section 118 the minutes will serve as evidence for the proceedings conducted in a meeting.

Presumptions. Where minutes are kept as per Section 118, it would be presumed, unless the contrary is proved, that the meeting was duly called and held. It would be presumed that all the proceedings at the meeting as recorded in minutes have duly taken place. It would also be presumed that all the appointments of directors, key managerial personnel (KMP), auditors or company secretary have been duly made.

Publication of reports of proceedings. No document purporting to be a report of proceedings of any General Meeting of a company shall be circulated or advertised at the expense of the company, unless it includes the matters required by section 118 to be contained in the minutes of the proceedings of such meeting.

Compliance with Secretarial Standards. It is necessary for every company to observe secretarial standards with respect to general meetings and board meetings, specified by the Institute of Company Secretaries of India (ICSI) and approved by the Central Government.

Punishment for contravention. If any default is committed in observing the provisions of this section the company shall be liable to a penalty of ` 25,000 and every officer in default shall be liable to a penalty of ` 5,000.

Punishment for tampering with minutes. Any person found guilty of tampering with the minutes shall be punishable with imprisonment upto 2 years and fine ranging from minimum ` 25,000 to ` 1 lakh.

Distinct minute book for each type of meeting. The company should maintain separate minute books for each type of meeting such as General meetings, Board meetings, Meetings of creditors, and Meetings of committees of board.

Preservation of minutes book. The minutes book of each meeting shall be preserved permanently at the registered office of the company, or at the such other place as may be approved by the board. The minutes book should be kept in the custody of the Company Secretary or any Director duly authorised by the Board. The book should be kept at the registered office of the company.

Inspection of minutes book. Any member of the company can inspect the book without paying any charges during the working hours, subject to reasonable restrictions as imposed by articles or a resolution at GM. If inspection is refused or copy is not furnished the company shall be liable to penalty of `25,000 and every officer in default shall be liable to penalty of ` 5,000 for each such refusal or default.

Report on Annual General Meeting

Section 121 of the Companies Act applies only to Public Companies. According to this section such companies are required to prepare a report on each AGM in the prescribed manner and a copy of it should be filed with the Registrar of Companies within 30 days of conclusion of AGM.

The Report should be prepared according to Rule 31 of the Companies (Management and Administration) Rules 2014. These rules are.

1.   **Preparation of Report**. The report should be prepared in addition to the minute of the annual general meeting (AGM) and should contain a fair and correct summary of the proceedings of the AGM.

2.   **Contents.** The report shall contain the following details:

(a)   The day, date, hour and venue of the AGM.

(b)   Confirmation with respect to appointment of Chairman of the meeting.

(c)   Number of members attending the meeting.

(d)   Confirmation of quorum.

(e)   Confirmation with respect to compliance of the Act and the rules, secretarial standards made there under with respect to calling, convening and conducting the meeting.

(f)   Business transacted at the meeting and result thereof.

(g)   Particulars with respect to any adjournment, postponement of meeting, change in venue.

(h)   Any other points relevant for inclusion in the report.

3.   **Signatures.** The report shall be signed by the Chairman of the meeting or in case of his inability to sign, by two directors of the company, one of whom shall be the managing director, if there is one and company secretary of the company.

4.   **Filing of Report**. A copy of the report of the AGM shall be filed with the Registrar in Form No. MGT – 15 within 30 days of the conclusion of the AGM along with the appropriate fees.

Non Applicability of provisions of provisions relating to General Meetings to One Person Companies (OPC).

1.   The provisions of Section 98 and Sections 100-101 of the Companies Act 2013 shall not apply to One Person Companies.

2.   In case of OPC, for the purpose of transacting any business at any GM by means of any resolution, it shall be sufficient if –

(a)   the resolution is communicated by the member to the company,

(b)   the resolution is entered in the minutes book and

(c)   The minutes book is signed and dated by the member.

3.   The date of signing the minutes book by the member shall be deemed to be the date of the meeting for all the purposes of the Act.

One Person Company

As per provision of section 2(62) of the Companies Act, 2013 defined (62) "one person company" means a company which has only one person as member.

FORMATION OF OPC [Rule 3]

Only a natural person who is an Indian citizen and resident in India-

- shall be eligible to incorporate a One Person Company;

- shall be a nominee for the sole member of a One Person Company.

70

PRIVILEGES AVAILABLE TO OPC

- The most significant reason for shareholders to incorporate the 'single-person company' is certainly the desire for the limited liability.

- Businesses currently run under the proprietorship model could get converted into OPCs without any difficulty.

- Mandatory rotation of auditor after expiry of maximum term is not applicable.

- One Person Company needs to have minimum of one director. It can have directors up to a maximum of 15 which can also be increased by passing a special resolution as in case of any other company.

- The provisions of Section 98 and Sections 100 to 111 (both inclusive), relating to holding of general meetings, shall not apply to a One Person Company.

- Minimum authorized share capital required for One Person Company having share capital is ` 1,00,000/-.

- Minimum and maximum number of members for One Person Company is one only.

CHAPTER 3

General Meetings

Meetings of shareholders are called General Meetings. Such meetings are very significant for the company because the Board of Directors are responsible for the day to day working of the company, but it is the shareholders who are the owners of the company. General Meetings provide the shareholders a platform where they can meet and deliberate on the working of the company.

Following are the various kinds of general meetings or meetings of shareholders.

Annual General Meeting

Section 96 of the Companies Act, 2013 applies to all companies except One Person Companies (OPC). Thus according to this section it is mandatory for all kinds of companies except One Person Company to hold an Annual General Meeting every year. It is very significant meeting for shareholders because they review and evaluate the overall progress of the company during the year. The Annual General Meeting is often called the 'ordinary general meeting' also since the 'ordinary business' as specified under Section 102(2)(a) is transacted at this meeting.

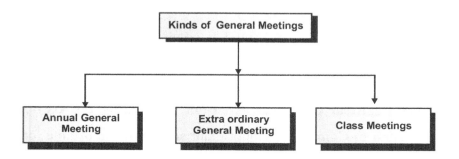

First AGM of a Company. After a company comes into existence through incorporation it is required to hold its first AGM. The time limit for such a meeting is nine months from the date of closing of the first financial year of the company. If a company holds its first AGM as per the above provisions it shall not be necessary for the company to hold any AGM in the year of its incorporation.

'Financial Year', means a period for which the financial statement of the company is made up. Financial Year means the period ending on 31st March every year. In case of a company incorporated on or after 1st January, the financial year means the period ending on 31st March of the following year.

Example 1: For a company incorporated on 31st December 2015, the financial year shall close on 31st March 2015 and Annual

General Meeting should be convened on or before 31st December 2015.

Example 2: For a company incorporated on 1st January 2015, the first financial year shall be closed on 31st March 2016 and Annual General Meeting should be convened on or before 31st December 2016.

Whether Registrar can grant extension for holding 1st AGM? The Registrar of Companies cannot grant any extension of time for holding the first AGM.

Subsequent Meetings. Following time limits are to be observed in any meeting other than the first AGM.

Such AGM should be held within 6 months of the close of the financial year.

Not more than 15 month shall elapse between the date of one AGM and that of the next, i.e. AGM should be held within 15 months of last AGM

Annual General Meeting should be held in each calendar year.

However, Registrar of Companies may, for any special reason, extend the time for holding the Annual General Meeting by any period not exceeding 3 months.

Example 1: If the last AGM had been held on 31st May 2015. The next AGM can be held on or before 31st August 2016, because the difference between two AGMs should not exceed 15 months.

Example 2: If the last AGM was held on 31st December 2015, the next AGM should be held on or before 30th September 2016, because the financial year ends on 31st March 2016 and the AGM should be held within 6 months of the closure of the relevant financial year which is 2015-2016 in this case.

Notice of Annual General Meeting: According to Section 101 of the Companies Act, 2013, a clear 21 days' notice should be given to each member. All the requirements as specified in the previous chapter regarding the length of notice should be complied with.

Time, Place and Day of Annual General Meeting: The Company should comply with the provisions of Section 96(2) relating to time, place and day of holding an annual general meeting. The AGM should be called on any day except on a day which falls on a National Holiday. The venue of the AGM should be registered office of the company but it can also be held at any other place within the city, town or village in which the registered office is situated. The meeting should be held during working hours i.e. 9AM to 6 PM.

Exemption by Central Government: The central government may exempt any company from the provisions contained in Section 96 (2) subject to conditions as the central government may impose.

Power of Tribunal to hold AGM: If any default is made in holding the annual general meeting of a company undersection 96, the Tribunal may, notwithstanding anything contained in this Act or the articles of the company, on the application of any member of the company, call, or direct the calling of, an annual general meeting of the company and give such ancillary or consequential directions as the Tribunal thinks expedient, provided that such directions may include a direction that one member of the company present in person or by proxy shall be deemed to constitute a meeting.

Penalty for default in holding AGM: If any default is made in holding a meeting of the company in accordance with section 96 or section 97 or section 98 or in complying with any directions of the Tribunal, the company and every officer of the company who is in default shall be punishable with fine which may extend to one lakh rupees and in the case of a continuing default, with a further fine which may extend to five thousand rupees for every day during which such default continues.

Duties of Company Secretary relating to Annual General Meeting

The Company Secretary is an important officer of the company whose duty is to ensure that the meeting is held according to the law and that all formalities and documentation is in order. He is responsible for making all the arrangements for holding the annual general meetings of the company. He is required to perform the following functions and duties in this connection.

(A) Before the Meeting

1.　As soon as final accounts are ready, the company secretary should give notice u/s 173(3) and arrange to convene a Board meeting. He should also invite the auditors for their report. In case of listed company an advance notice should be given to the stock exchange. (In case of listed company prior intimation should to be sent to stock exchange of the Board meeting where recommendation of dividend is proposed to be considered at least 2 working days in advance vide clause 19 of listing agreement. If the Auditors' report contains any reservations qualification or adverse remarks, the Board's Report must contain explanations.)

The following business is required to be conducted at the board meeting.

(a)　To consider and discuss the report of Audit Committee on the Annual accounts.

(b)　To approve the accounts and authorise signing of accounts.

(c)　To secure Auditor's report on the accounts.

(d)   To approve the draft of the Board's Report in compliance with the provisions of Section 134 of the Act and to authorise the Chairman to sign the Report on behalf of the Board.

(e)   To consider the payment of dividend, if any, in case it is to be declared in the Annual General Meeting

(f)   To fix time, date and place for the annual general meeting, approve the draft notice and also authorise the Secretary to issue Notice for the meeting. The Notice must contain Ordinary Business in accordance with the provisions of Section 102 of the Act, While fixing the time, date and place for the annual general meeting, care should be taken that the time should be between 9 am to 6 pm, the date should not be a National holiday, and the place should be either the registered office of the company or some other place within the same city, town or village in which the registered office of the company is situated.

(g)   To consider the closure of the Register of Members and the Share Transfer Books of the Company in compliance with the provisions of Section 91 of the Act and to authorise the Secretary to arrange for its publication in a newspaper. In case of listed company, a notice in advance of at least 7 working days should be sent to the stock exchange(s) about the proposed dates for such closure and also to comply with the requirement of stock exchange for book closure.

2.   Immediately after the Board meeting, the stock exchanges should be informed of the dividends and/or cash bonuses recommended by the Board and to the shareholders in their Report, and financial information like the total turnover, gross profit/loss, provision for depreciation, tax provision and net profit/loss, for the year with comparative figures of the last year and the amounts appropriated from reserves and accumulated profits of the previous years' etc. Such intimation has to be sent within 15 minutes of closure of the Board meeting.

3.   To arrange for the publication in a newspaper of at least 7 days previous notice of closure of the Register of Members and the Share Transfer Books as per Section 91 of the Act.

4.   In case of listed company, close the registers for the period as advertised and inform all the stock exchanges by giving a notice in advance of at least 7 working days.

5.   To arrange for the printing of the balance sheet, profit and loss account, reports of the directors and of the auditors and the notice for the meeting.

6.   To issue notice to the shareholders, at least 21 clear days before the date of annual general meeting and where it is to be sent by post, it should be posted 48 hours still earlier in terms of section 101. Notice of the meeting must also be sent to the directors (whether member or not), auditors and stock exchanges.

7.   If the directors decide for the publication of the Chairman's statement, make arrangements for the same.

8.   In case of listed company, send six copies of the directors' report, balance sheet and profit and loss account and three copies of the notices to such stock exchange(s) and one copy of each of them to all other recognised stock exchanges in India.

9.   Check proxies with the Register of Members as and when they are received, from day to day, so that an up-to-date position is available till the date of the meeting.

10.   To arrange for the printing of attendance slips or attendance register and ballot papers.

11.   In consultation with the chairman or the Managing Director, prepare a detailed agenda for the meeting.

12.   To prepare Dividend List from the Register of Members/beneficial owners, as on the last date of the closure of the Register of Members and the Share Transfer Books.

13.   To make arrangement for the printing of a combined document containing "Notice of Dividend" and" Dividend Warrant".

(B) At the Meeting

1.   To arrange for the collection of admission slips or in the alternative to get the Attendance Register signed by the

shareholders, and to make them comfortable in their seats, and to look to the comfort and convenience of the directors and the chairman.

2.   To help the Chairman in ascertaining quorum.

3.   To read out the notice of the meeting if advised by the Chairman.

4.   To read out the Auditor's Report, if advised by the Chairman, when the item relating to adoption of accounts is taken up for consideration.

5.   To produce copies of Memorandum and Articles of Association of the company.

6.   To help the Chairman in the conduct of the meeting, particularly in the conduct of poll, counting of votes etc.

7.   To supply to the Chairman any information which he may require in connection with the queries raised by the shareholders relating to accounts and other connected matters.

8.   Give advance information to the members who are to propose and second the resolutions to be passed at the meeting.

9.   To take notes of the proceedings for the purpose of preparing minutes thereof.

10. To keep at the meeting Register of Members, Minutes Book of the general meeting containing minutes of the previous annual general meeting(s), copies of the accounts, notice of the meeting and reports of the directors and of the auditors.

11. To ensure that the Chairman of the Audit Committee is present at annual general meeting to provide any clarification on matters relating to audit and to answer shareholders' queries.

(C) After the Meeting

1. To prepare minutes of the proceedings.

2. To record the minutes of the meeting and get them signed by the Chairman within thirty days of the meeting.

3. To send intimation of appointment/re-appointment of directors. File Form DIR-12 with the Registrar of Companies within 30 days of appointment along with filing fee.

4. To send intimation of appointment/re-appointment of auditors.

5. To file copies of the special and other resolutions, if any, passed at the meeting, along with Form MGT-14 with the Registrar of Companies, within thirty days of the meeting.

6. To file balance sheet, profit and loss account, reports of the directors and the auditors and the notice of the meeting in

Form AOC-4 within thirty days of the meeting. In case of companies covered under XBRL filing, it should be ensured that the annual accounts are filed in XBRL format. Ensure that a copy of Secretarial Audit Report obtained from a Secretary in whole time practice as required under Section 204(1) of the Act, if any, is filed with Registrar of Companies within 30 days from the date of annual general meeting. In case of listed company, send a copy of the proceedings of the annual general meeting to the stock exchange.

7.   Deposit dividend distribution tax at the applicable rate within the prescribed time limit under Income tax Act, 1961.

8.   Where the company has invited public deposits, a copy of the Balance sheet shall be forwarded to the RBI.

9.   To open a separate bank account known as "Dividend Account for the year........" and to deposit the total amount of dividend within five days from the date of declaration of dividend.

10.   To get the Dividend Warrants and Notice of Dividend signed by authorised persons.

11.   To despatch Dividend Warrants together with the Notice of Dividend to the shareholders within thirty days of the declaration of dividend after making arrangement with the banker for payment of dividend warrants at prescribed number of branches at par.

12.   To file along with the prescribed filing fee, Annual Return in Schedule V to the Companies Act as an attachment to Form MGT – 7 with the Registrar of Companies within sixty days of the meeting prepared as at the date of the annual general meeting, as required by Section 92 of the Companies Act, 1956. The Certificate of Company Secretary shall be in Form MGT – 8 and abstract of annual return shall be attached with Board Report in Form MGT – 9. Ensure that in the case of listed company, the annual return is also signed by a Company Secretary in whole time practice.

13.   To take action on other decisions of the shareholders.

14.   If the company is listed then to submit to the stock exchange, within 48 hours of conclusion of annual general meeting, details regarding the voting results in the following format as prescribed in clause 35 A of the listing agreement:-

Date of the AGM/EGM: _____

Total number of shareholders on record date:

No. of Shareholders present in the meeting either in person or through proxy:

Promoters and Promoter Group: Public:

No. of Shareholders attended the meeting through Video Conferencing

Promoters and Promoter Group: Public:

(Agenda-wise)

Detail of the Agenda:

Resolution required: (Ordinary/Special)

Mode of voting: (Show of hands/Poll/Postal ballot/E-voting)

Extraordinary General Meeting (Section 100 of Companies Act 2013)

Every general meeting of the company other than an Annual General Meeting is known as 'Extraordinary General Meeting' (EGM). Such meetings can be convened by the company at any time. The business transacted at such meetings are of an extraordinary nature which cannot be postponed till the next AGM for example issues of debentures, alteration in memorandum or articles etc. All business at such meetings are known as 'special business'. In other words 'ordinary business' cannot be transacted at EGM.

Power to call EGM

An EGM may be called by:-

1.   The Board of Directors

2.   By Members on a valid requisition

3.   By the Tribunal (u/s 98 of Companies Act, 2013)

1.   EGM called by the Board.

The board may whenever it desires may convene an EGM. Such action of the Board of Directors to call a meeting on its own is known as 'Suo Motu' action.

2.   EGM called on a requisition of members.

Such meetings may be of two kinds

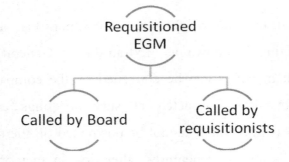

According to the Companies Act only members having a specified amount of paid up equity share capital or voting power can requisition an extraordinary general meeting. If this requirement is not met, the requisition will not be valid. Following is the number of members who can make a requisition.

S.No.	Kind of Company	Amount of paid up share capital required.
1.	Company having share capital	Member/s holding at least $1/10^{th}$ of paid up equity share capital.
2.	Company not having share capital	Member/s holding at least $1/10^{th}$ of total voting power.

Essentials of a valid requisition made by members

- The requisition should specify the matters for the consideration of which EGM is to be called. But absence of the reasons for calling of the EGM does not invalidate the meeting.

  o The requisition should be signed by:

  o all the requisitionists, or

  o a requisitionists duly authorised, by all other requisitionists.

- The requisition should be deposited at the registered office of the company.

- The requisition should be in writing. It may be sent by the following modes:

  o By means of a written requisition.

  o By sending a request in electronic form and attaching a scanned copy of a duly signed requisition.

- The members making the requisition may propose a date for convening the EGM. But the requisition should be deposited at least 21 days before the proposed date.

A. EGM called by Board of Directors

- When a valid requisition is received by the Board it should hold the EGM within 21 days and the meeting should not be held later than 45 days from the date of deposit of requisition.

- The Board should give the notice regarding the holding of the meeting to all the members whose name appears in the Register of members. Such notice should be given within 3 days of receipt of a valid requisition.

B. EGM called by the requisitionists

Where the Board fails to conduct the EGM, the requisitionists can proceed to hold the meeting on their own.

- Such a meeting should be held within 3 months from the date of deposit of resolution.

- The requisitionists can proceed to call the meeting in the same manner as is called by the Board.

- The requisitionists are entitled to receive a list of members. The list should be made as on 21 days from the receipt of the requisition for calling EGM together with such changes as may have occurred upto the 45th day from the date of receipt of requisition.

- The meeting should be held on a working day, during business hours and at the registered office of the company or at any other place in the same city or town in which the registered office is situated.

- The notice of the meeting should be given all members either through speed post, or registered post, or electronic mode. If through accidental omission notice is not given to any member the proceedings of the EGM cannot be invalidated.

- The notice should disclose the place, date, day and hour of the EGM along with the agenda and resolution to be passed.

- The requisitionists are entitled to recover reasonable expenses incurred on holding the EGM, which will ultimately be recovered from the remuneration of directors who failed to hold the meeting.

Time frame for holding EGM called by under section 100

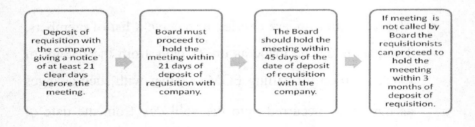

Place of holding EGM on the requisition of members if not held by Board:

Judicial pronouncements.

Bharat Commerce and Industries Ltd vs Registrar of Companies

An EGM may be held at any place, even though such place is outside the State in which registered office of the company situated.

R. Chettiar vs M. Chettiar

Where the Board failed to call the EGM, and meetings were generally held in the registered office of the company, but the registered office was not made available to the requisitionists, the EGM held elsewhere was held to be valid.

Power of Tribunal to call meetings of members (Section 98 of the Companies Act, 2013).

Where for any reason it becomes impracticable to hold an EGM, National Company Law Tribunal (NCLT), may order the holding of an EGM if:

(a) An application is made by a member, or

(b) An application is made by a director, or

(c) On its own (Suo Moto).

The NCLT may give such ancillary or consequential directions as it thinks fit (including a direction that one member present in person or proxy shall be quorum.

Duties of Company Secretary relating to Extraordinary General Meeting

The Company Secretary shall take care of all the provisions of Section 100, Section 98 of the Companies Act along with the relevant Secretarial Standards and other matters relating to holding of Extraordinary General Meeting. Precisely he should take care of the following matters.

A. Before the meeting

1. If the meeting is being convened by the Board suo motu, he advises the Board of the urgency of the meeting. He should inform the Board that the issues are of such a nature that they cannot be deferred to the next annual general meeting. He should thereafter urge the members of the Board to convene a Board meeting in consultation with the Chairman in order to fix the date, time, place and business for the proposed EGM.

2. If the meeting is being called on the requisition of the members he will have to see that the members who have made the requisition are eligible as per the provisions of the Act and whether it has been received in the stipulated time. He will therefore inform the Board about the requisition and the legal formalities relating to such a meeting.

3.   If the Board decides to hold the meeting, the secretary should assist the Board in preparing the draft resolutions and Explanatory notes.

4.   The secretary will then draft a notice after taking the following points into consideration

- The notice should mention that this is an EGM.

- It should specify whether it is a Meeting called by the Board or is a Requisitioned Meeting.

- The notice should state the resolutions to be passed in the meeting.

- The notice should be accompanied by explanatory statement mentioning all material facts.

5.   The Secretary should arrange for the printing of the notices, explanatory statement, proxy forms and admission slips.

6.   Thereafter the Secretary will arrange to get the notices posted to the registered address of each member and/or arrange to get them electronically delivered. He will require to ensure that 21 clear days' notice has been given. The notice should

also be inserted as an advertisement in an English and a Vernacular newspaper.

7.   The Secretary should also prepare the agenda of the meeting in consultation with the chairman.

8.   He should prepare a list of proxies and make arrangements for poll.

9.   The secretary should make necessary seating arrangements. He should make arrangements in such a manner that ordinary shareholders, preference shareholders and proxies are seated separately.

B. At the meeting

1.   To arrange for the collection of admission slips or in the alternative to get the Attendance Register signed by the shareholders, and to make them comfortable in their seats, and to look to the comfort and convenience of the directors and the chairman.

2.   To help the Chairman in ascertaining quorum.

3.   To read out the notice of the meeting if advised by the Chairman.

4.   To give necessary explanations and supply documents as demanded by the chairman.

5.   To help the Chairman in the conduct of the meeting, particularly in the conduct of poll, counting of votes etc.

6.   To supply to the Chairman any information which he may require in connection with the queries raised by the shareholders relating to accounts and other connected matters.

7.   Give advance information to the members who are to propose and second the resolutions to be passed at the meeting.

8.   To take notes of the proceedings for the purpose of preparing minutes thereof.

9.   To keep at the meeting Register of Members, Minutes Book of the extraordinary general ready.

C. After the meeting

1. To prepare minutes of the proceedings.

2. To record the minutes of the meeting and get them signed by the Chairman within thirty days of the meeting.

3. To take action on decisions of the EGM.

4. The Secretary has to ensure that a copy of every special resolution (together with explanatory statement) is filed with the Registrar within 30 days of passing the special resolution.

Class Meetings

In case the share capital of a company is divided into different classes of shares and the company wants to make any variation in the rights attached to shares of any particular class, meetings of different classes of shareholders may have to be held. Class meeting is an exception to the general rule that at least two persons should meet to constitute a meeting. In case of class meetings even a single person may belong to a class and in that case the single person can constitute a valid meeting.

Regulation 6 of the Table F of Schedule I of the Act provides as under:

(a)   If at any time the share capital is divided into different classes of shares, the rights attached to any class (unless otherwise provided by the terms of issue of the shares of that class) may, subject to the provisions of section 48, and whether or not the company is being wound up, be varied with the consent in writing of the holders of three-fourths of the issued shares of that class, or with the sanction of a special resolution passed at a separate meeting of the holders of the shares of that class.

(b)   To every such separate meeting, the provisions of these regulations relating to general meetings shall mutatis mutandis apply, but so that the necessary quorum shall be at least two persons holding at least one-third of the issued shares of the class in question. The articles of companies will have to be suitably modified or incorporated depending on the needs of each case on the above lines.

A class meeting will have to be convened by the Board of directors in the same manner as calling any other extraordinary general meeting. The Board will authorise the secretary or any other competent officer to issue the notice. The other procedures/provisions relating to service of notice, persons to whom notice should be given, chairman, voting, proxy, minutes, poll etc. are similar to those discussed earlier in case of general meetings. Further if the company is listed then it has to submit to the stock exchange, within 48 hours of conclusion of class. meeting, details regarding the voting results in the format prescribed in clause 35 A of the listing agreement.

Specimen of formats

NOTICE OF ANNUAL GENERAL MEETING XYZ LIMITED.

Registered Office :..

NOTICE is hereby given that the Second Annual General Meeting of the Members of XYZ Limited will be held on

Tuesday, the 7th October, 2014, at 3:30 p.m. at _____ (address) to transact the following business:

Ordinary Business:

1. To receive, consider and adopt the Audited Balance Sheet as at March 31, 2014, the Profit & Loss Account for the year ended on that date together with the Schedules and Notes attached thereto, alongwith the Reports of the Auditors and Directors thereon.

2. To declare dividend.

3. To appoint a Director in place of Mr X, who retires by rotation and being eligible, offers himself for reappointment.

4. To appoint a Director in place of Mr Y, who retires by rotation and being eligible, offers himself for reappointment.

5. To appoint a Director in place of Mr Z, who retires by rotation and being eligible, offers himself for reappointment.

6. To appoint Auditors and to fix their remuneration.

Special Business:

Appointment of Director

7. To consider and, if thought fit, to pass, with or without modifications, the following Resolution as an Ordinary

Resolution:

"RESOLVED THAT Mr D, who was appointed as an Additional Director by the Board of Directors of the Company pursuant to sub section (1) of Section 161 of the Companies Act,

2013 and Article ___ of the Articles of Association of the Company and who holds office only upto the date of this Annual General Meeting and in respect of whom the Company has received a Notice in writing, under Section 160 of the Companies Act, 2013, from a Member signifying his intention to propose Mr. D as a candidate for the office of a Director of the Company, together with the deposit of one lakh rupees be and is hereby appointed a Director of the Company liable to retire by rotation."

Delisting of securities

8. To consider and, if thought fit, to pass the following Resolution as a Special Resolution:

"RESOLVED THAT, subject to the provisions of the Securities Contracts (Regulation) Act, 1956, and the Securities and Exchange of Board of India Act, 1992 and the rules framed thereunder and other applicable laws, rules and regulations and guidelines and subject to such other approvals, permission and sanctions as may be necessary and subject to such conditions as may be prescribed by The Securities and Exchange Board of India and Stock Exchanges while granting such approvals, permission and sanctions which may be agreed to by the Board of Directors of the Company, which expression shall be deemed to include any Committee of the Board for the time being exercising the powers conferred by the Board, the consent of the Company be and is hereby accorded to the Board to voluntarily de-list the equity shares

99

of the Company from The Stock Exchange - Ahmedabad, The Calcutta Stock Exchange Association Limited and The Ludhiana Stock Exchange Association Limited.

"RESOLVED FURTHER THAT the Board be and is hereby authorised to do all acts, deeds and things as it may in its absolute discretion deem necessary and appropriate to give effect to the above resolution."

By order of the Board of Directors

PQR

Company Secretary

Place : New Delhi

Date : 26th August 2014.

Notes:

1.   The explanatory statement pursuant to Section 102 of the Companies Act, 2013 relating to special business to be transacted at the Meeting is annexed.

2.   A Member entitled to attend and vote at the Meeting is entitled to appoint a Proxy to attend and, on a poll, to vote instead of himself and the Proxy need not be a Member of the Company. Proxies, in order to be effective, must be received at the

Registered Office of the Company not less than forty-eight hours before the time fixed for the Meeting. A proxy form is enclosed.

3.   All documents referred to in the Notice and accompanying explanatory statement are open for inspection at the Registered Office of the Company on all working days of the Company between 11:00 a.m. and 1:00 p.m. upto the date of the Annual General Meeting and at the venue of the Meeting for the duration of the Meeting.

4.   The Register of Members and Share Transfer Books will remain closed from Tuesday, 30th September 2014 to Tuesday, 7th October 2014 (both days inclusive).

5.   The dividend on shares, if declared at the Meeting, will be paid within thirty days from the date of declaration to those Members or their mandatees whose names appear:

(a)   as beneficial owners as on Tuesday, 7th October 2014, as per the lists to be furnished by NSDL/CDSL, in respect of shares held in electronic form; and

(b)   as Members in the Register of Members of the Company after giving effect to valid share transfers in physical form lodged with the Company on or before Tuesday, 7th October 2014.

6.   Pursuant to Section 123 of the Companies Act, 2013, dividend for the financial year ended 31st March 2007, which remains unclaimed for a period of seven years, will be transferred to the Investor Education &Protection Fund of the Central Government. Members who have not encashed their dividend warrants in respect of the said dividend are requested to make their claim to the Share Department of the Company at the Registered Office of the Company or to the Registrars & Share Transfer Agents of the Company at...................................... (address). It may be noted that once the amounts in the unpaid dividend accounts are transferred to the Investor Education and Protection Fund of the Central Government, no claim shall lie against the Fund or the Company in respect thereof and the Members would lose their right to claim such dividend.

7.   The Company has already transferred unclaimed dividend to the General Revenue Account of the Central Government. Members who have so far not claimed or collected their dividends for the said period may claim their dividend from the Registrar of Companies, NCT of Delhi, by submitting an application in the prescribed form.

8.   Members are requested to notify the change in their address to the Company and always quote their Folio Numbers or DP ID and Client ID Numbers in all correspondence with the Company. In respect of holding in electronic form, Members are

requested to notify any change of address to their respective Depository Participants.

9.   Members holding shares in electronic form may please note that their bank details as furnished to the respective Depositories will be printed on their dividend warrants as per the applicable regulations. The Company will not entertain any direct request from such Members for deletion or change of such bank details. Instructions, if any, already given by Members in respect of shares held in physical form will not be automatically applicable to the dividend paid on shares in electronic form.

10.   Any query relating to Accounts must be sent to the Company's Registered Office at least seven days before the date of the Meeting.

11.   With a view to serving the Members better and for administrative convenience, an attempt has been made to consolidate multiple folios. Members who hold shares in identical names and in the same order of names in more than one folio are requested to write to the Company to consolidate their holdings in one folio.

12.   Members who still hold shares certificates in physical form are advised to dematerialise their share holding to avail the benefits of dematerialisation, which include easy liquidity (since trading is permitted in dematerialised form only), electronic

transfer, savings in stamp duty and elimination of any possibility of loss of documents and bad deliveries.

13.   Members can avail of the nomination facility under Section 72 of the Companies Act by filing relevant Forms, with the Company. Blank forms will be supplied on request.

14.   As per the provisions of the Income Tax Act, 1961, tax is required to be deducted at source if the gross amount of dividend payable to a resident individual shareholder during the financial year exceeds ' 2,500. Resident individual shareholders who are likely to receive dividend amounting to more than ' 2,500 during the financial year and whose total estimated income from dividend as provided in Section 197 A (1B) of the Income Tax Act, 1961, during such financial year is not likely to exceed ' 50,000 can claim gross dividend without deduction of tax at source by submitting a declaration in Form 15 G (in duplicate) with the Company's Share Department at its Registered Office or with the Company's Registrars & Share Transfer Agents before 19th September 2014. Please note that it would not be possible for the Company to act upon 15 G declarations received thereafter As per the provisions of the Income Tax Act, 1961, every person from whose income any tax is to be deducted at source is mandatorily required to intimate Permanent Account Number (PAN) to the person responsible for deducting such tax at source. In case the Income Tax Department has not allotted PAN, the person is required to intimate General Index Register Number (GIR No.).

Members whose dividend will be liable to deduction of tax at source are requested to intimate PAN/GIR No. to the Company's Share Department or the Company's Registrars & Share Transfer Agents before 19th September 2014.

15.   In accordance with the provisions of Article _____ of the Articles of Association of the Company, Mr.X, Mr. Y and Mr. Z will retire by rotation at the Annual General Meeting and, being eligible, offer themselves for re-election. Further, Mr. D was appointed as an Additional Director and retires at the Annual General Meeting and the Company has received a notice for his reappointment at the Annual General Meeting. Additional information pursuant to Clause 49 of the Listing Agreement with Stock Exchanges, in respect of Directors seeking election, those retiring by rotation and seeking reappointment at the Annual General Meeting is given elsewhere in the Annual Report.

EXPLANATORY STATEMENT

As required by Section 102 of the Companies Act, 2013, the following explanatory statement sets out all material facts relating to the business mentioned under Item Nos. 7 and 8 of the accompanying Notice dated 26th August 2014.

Item No. 7

Appointment of Director

Mr. D was appointed by the Board of Directors of the Company on 15th April, 2014 as an additional Director and, as per the provisions of Section 161(1) of the Companies Act, 2013, he holds office as a Director up to the date of this Annual General Meeting. The Company has received a Notice from a Member alongwith a deposit of ?100,000 signifying his intention to propose the appointment of Mr. D as a Director of the Company.

The Directors commend the passing of the resolution at Item No. 7

Mr. D may be deemed to be concerned or interested in the resolution relating to his appointment.

Item No. 8

Delisting of Securities

The equity shares of the Company are listed on the following stock exchanges: The Stock Exchange, Mumbai (BSE)

The National Stock Exchange of India Limited (NSE) The Delhi Stock Exchange Association (DSE)

The Stock Exchange - Ahmedabad (ASE)

The Ludhiana Stock Exchange Association Limited (LSE)

The Calcutta Stock Exchange Association Limited (CSE)

With the extensive connectivity of the BSE and NSE, investors have access to dealings in the equity shares of the Company all over the country. The bulk of the trading in the equity shares of the Company takes place on the BSE and NSE only. Trading, if any, on the other stock exchanges is negligible and the listing fees paid to these other stock exchanges are dis-proportionately high as compared to the trading volumes. As part of the cost reduction measures and to protect the investors' funds, it is proposed to voluntarily delist the equity shares of the Company from the Stock Exchanges at Ahmedabad, Ludhiana and Calcutta. However, the shares will continue to be listed at DSE, being the principal stock exchange. The proposed delisting of equity shares will not adversely affect the investors, as the Company's equity shares will continue to be listed on the BSE, NSE and the principal stock exchange DSE. The delisting will take effect after all approvals, permission and sanctions are received. Since the approval of Members is required for such voluntary delisting by way of a Special Resolution, the Directors commend the passing of the Special Resolution at Item No. 8. None of the Directors of the Company is deemed to be concerned or interested in the above resolution. By order of the Board of Directors PQR Company Secretary

Place : New Delhi

Date : 26th August 2014.

ATTENDANCE SLIP

XYZ LIMITED

Registered Office :...

Members attending the Meeting in person or by Proxy or as Authorised Representatives are requested to complete this attendance slip and hand it over at the entrance of the Meeting hall.

I hereby record my presence at the SECOND ANNUAL GENERAL MEETING of XYZ LIMITED at............................

(address), at 3:30 p.m. on Tuesday, 7th October, 2014.

Full name of the Shareholder Signature

Folio No.: / DP ID No.: & Client ID No.:

Full name of Proxy/Authorised Signature of Proxy/Authorised

Representative Representative

(in capital letters)

Note : Shareholder/Proxy holder/Authorised Representative desiring to attend the Meeting should bring his copy of the Annual Report to the Meeting.

FORM OF PROXY

XYZ LIMITED

Registered Office :...

I/We....................................., being a Member(s) of XYZ LIMITED, hereby appoint the following as my/our Proxy to attend on my/our behalf at the .... Annual General Meeting/General Meeting of the Company, to be held on.................................. at..................... a.m./p.m. and at any adjournment thereof:

1.   Mr./Ms............................   (Name)..........................
(Signature), or failing him -

2.   Mr./Ms...........................   (Name)...........................
(Signature), or failing him -

3.   Mr./Ms....................................
(Name)................................... (Signature), or failing him -

**I/We direct my/our Proxy to vote on the Resolutions in the manner as indicated below :

Resolutions For Against

Resolution No. 1. (To specify)

Resolution No. 2. (To specify)

Resolution No. 3. (To specify)

Resolution No. 4. (To specify)

Number of Shares held

Affix

Revenue

Stamp

Signed this.................................. day of...................................
2014. Reference Folio No./DP ID & Client ID

Signature(s) of Members(s)

(1)....................................

(2)....................................

(3)....................................

Notes :

1.   The Proxy, to be effective, must be received at the Registered Office of the Company not less than forty eight hours before the time fixed for the Meeting.

2.   A Proxy need not be a Member of the Company.

3.   In the case of joint holders, the vote of the senior who tenders the vote, whether in person or by proxy, shall be accepted to the exclusion of the vote of the other joint holder(s). Seniority shall be determined by the order in which the names stand in the Register of Members.

4.   This form of Proxy confers authority on the holder to demand or join in demanding a poll.

5.   The submission by a Member of this Proxy form will not preclude such Member from attending in person and voting at the Meeting.

6.   **This is optional. Please put a tick mark ( ) in the appropriate column against the Resolution indicated in the box. If a Member leaves the "For" or "Against" column blank against any or all Resolutions, the Proxy will be entitled to vote in the manner he thinks appropriate. If a Member wishes to abstain from voting on a particular Resolution, he should write "abstain" across the boxes against that Resolution.

7.   In case a Member wishes his votes to be used differently, he should indicate the number of shares under the columns "For" and "Against", as appropriate.

NOTICE IN NEWSPAPERS OF ANNUAL GENERAL MEETING

XYZ LIMITED

Registered Office :..

NOTICE is hereby given that the Second Annual General Meeting of the Company will be held on Tuesday, 7th October 2014 at 3:30 p.m. at.. (address) to transact the business as set out in the Notice dated 8th September, 2014 a copy of which, along with the relative explanatory statement, has been posted to the Members of the Company at their address registered with the Company, together with the Annual Report and accounts for the year ended 31st March 2014.

The Register of Members and the Share Transfer Books will remain closed from the 30th September 2014 to 7th October, 2014 (both days inclusive) for the purpose of the Annual General Meeting and payment of dividend, if declared at the Meeting.

Dividend, if declared, will be payable to those Members whose names appear on the Register of Members of the Company on 7th October 2014. In respect of shares held in electronic form, dividend will be payable on the basis of beneficial ownership as per details furnished on 7th

October, 2014 by NSDL/CDSL.

A Member entitled to attend and vote at the Meeting is entitled to appoint a Proxy to attend and, on a poll, to vote instead of himself and the Proxy need not be a Member of the Company. Proxies, in order to be effective, must be received at the Registered Office of the Company not less than forty-eight hours before the time fixed for the

Meeting.

By order of the Board of Directors

PQR Company Secretary

Place : New Delhi.

SPECIMEN MINUTES OF ANNUAL GENERAL MEETING OF MEMBERS

XYZ LIMITED

MINUTES OF THE PROCEEDINGS OF THE SECOND ANNUAL GENERAL MEETING OF XYZ LIMITED

HELD ON TUESDAY, 7th October, 2014 AT 3:30 p.m. AT_____ (ADDRESS)

The following were present:

1. Mr. W (in the Chair)

2. Mr. B (Director and Member)

3. Mr. C (Director)

4. Mr. D (Director and Member)

5. Mr. E. (Director, Chairman of Audit Committee)

6. Mr. F (Company Secretary)

7. _____ (Members present in person) [state number]

8. _____ (Members present by Proxy) [state number]

Mr. G, Partner of M/s_____, Secretary, was also present.

CHAIRMAN

In accordance with Article _____ of the Articles of Association, Mr. W, Chairman of the Board of Directors, took Chartered Accountants, Auditors of the Company, was present. Mr. H, PractisingCompany the Chair.

OR

{*Mr. B was elected Chairman of the Meeting, in terms of Article _____ of the Articles of Association of the Company*}.

The Chairman welcomed the Members and introduced the Directors seated on the dais.

The Chairman declared that the requisite Quorum was present and called the Meeting to order. The Register of Directors' shareholdings was placed at the Meeting and was available for inspection. With the consent of the Members present, the Notice convening the Annual General Meeting of the Company was taken as read. The Chairman requested the Company Secretary to read the Auditors' Report.

After the Auditor's Report had been read, the Chairman delivered his speech.

The business of the Meeting as per the Notice thereof was thereafter taken up item wise.

1.   Adoption of Accounts

The Chairman requested Mr. _____ to read the Ordinary Resolution for the adoption of the Accounts for the year ended 31st March 2014 and Mr._____ read out the Ordinary Resolution as follows:

"RESOLVED THAT the audited Balance Sheet of the Company as at 31st March 2014 and the Profit and Loss Account of the Company for the financial year ended on that date, together with the Schedules and Notes attached thereto, along with the Reports thereon of the Directors and the Auditors, as circulated to the Members and laid before the Meeting, be and are hereby approved and adopted."

After the above Resolution was proposed and seconded, but before it was put to the vote, the Chairman invited Members (other than those present by Proxy) to make observations and comments, if any, on the Report and

Accounts, as well as on the other Resolutions set out in the Notice convening the Meeting.

Some Members made their observations and comments and raised queries on the Annual Report and Accounts and other items set out in the Notice and the Chairman answered their queries.

Before putting the Resolution to vote, the Chairman reminded the Meeting that Proxies were not eligible to vote on a show of hands. Thereafter, the Chairman put the Resolution for the adoption of the Accounts and the Reports thereon to the vote as an Ordinary Resolution.

On a show of hands, the Chairman declared the aforesaid Ordinary Resolution carried by the requisite majority.

2.   Declaration of Dividend

Mr. _____ read the following Resolution as an Ordinary Resolution:

"RESOLVED THAT the dividend @ ` 2 on the equity shares of ` 10 each, fully paid-up, be and is hereby declared for payment, after deduction of tax at source, if any, to those Members whose names appear on the Company's Register of Members on Tuesday, 24th September 2014".

The Resolution was proposed by Mr. _____ and seconded by Mr._____, and was put to the vote as an Ordinary Resolution.

On a show of hands, the Chairman declared the aforesaid Ordinary Resolution carried unanimously.

3.   Appointment of Director

Proposed by : Mr. _____

Seconded by : Mr. _____

The following Resolution having been proposed and seconded by the aforementioned two Members, was put to the vote as an Ordinary Resolution:

"RESOLVED THAT, pursuant to Section 152 (6)(a) of the Companies Act, 2014, Mr. A, who retires by rotation and, being eligible for re-appointment, offers himself for re-appointment, be and is hereby re-appointed as a Director of the Company and that his period of office be liable to determination by retirement of Directors by rotation."

On a show of hands, the Chairman declared the aforesaid Ordinary Resolution carried unanimously.

4.   Appointment of Director

Proposed by : Mr. _____

Seconded by : Mr. _____

The following Resolution having been proposed and seconded by the aforementioned two Members, was put to the vote as an Ordinary Resolution:

"RESOLVED THAT, pursuant to Section Section 152 (6)(a) of the Companies Act, 2013, Mr. B, who retires by rotation and, being eligible for re-appointment, offers himself for re-appointment, be and is hereby re-appointed as a Director of the Company and that his period of office be liable to determination by retirement of Directors by rotation.

5.   Appointment of Director

Proposed by : Mr. _____

Seconded by : Mr. _____

The following Resolution having been proposed and seconded by the aforementioned two Members, was put to the vote as an Ordinary Resolution:

"RESOLVED THAT, pursuant to Section 152 (6)(a) of the Companies Act, 2014, Mr. A, who retires by rotation and, being eligible for re-appointment, offers himself for re-appointment, be and is hereby re-appointed as a Director of the Company and that his period of office be liable to determination by retirement of Directors by rotation."

On a show of hands, the Chairman declared the aforesaid Ordinary Resolution carried unanimously.

6.   Appointment of Director

Proposed by : Mr. _____

Seconded by : Mr. _____

The following Resolution having been proposed and seconded by the aforementioned two Members, was put to the vote as an Ordinary Resolution:

"RESOLVED THAT, pursuant to Section Section 152 (6)(a) of the Companies Act, 2013, Mr. B, who retires by rotation and, being eligible for re-appointment, offers himself for re-appointment, be and is hereby re-appointed as a Director of the Company and that his period of office be liable to determination by retirement of Directors by rotation."

On a show of hands, the Chairman declared the aforesaid Ordinary Resolution carried unanimously.

7.   Appointment of Auditors

Proposed by : Mr. _____

Seconded by : Mr. _____

The following Resolution having been proposed and seconded by the aforementioned two Members, was put to the vote as an Ordinary Resolution:

"RESOLVED   THAT M/s._____, Chartered Accountants, _____, be and are hereby re-appointed as Auditors of the Company to hold office from the conclusion of this Meeting until the conclusion of the next Annual General Meeting of the Company on a remuneration of ' _____, plus applicable service tax and other out of pocket expenses incurred for the purposes of the audit".

On a show of hands, the Chairman declared the aforesaid Ordinary Resolution carried unanimously.

8.   Appointment of Director

Proposed by : Mr. _____

Seconded by : Mr. _____

The following Resolution having been proposed and seconded by the aforementioned two Members, was put to the vote as an Ordinary Resolution:

"RESOLVED THAT Mr. D who was appointed as an Additional Director by the Board under Section 161(1) of the Companies Act, 2013 and Article ___ of the Articles of Association of the Company and who holds office only upto the date of this Annual General Meeting and in respect of whom the Company has received a Notice in writing, under Section 160 of the Companies Act, 2013, from a Member signifying his intention to propose Mr. D as a candidate for the office of a Director of the Company, together with the prescribed deposit be and is hereby appointed a Director of the Company liable to retire by rotation."

On a show of hands, the Chairman declared the aforesaid Ordinary Resolution carried unanimously.

9.   Delisting of Securities – Special Resolution

        Proposed by : Mr. _____

        Seconded by : Mr. _____

The following Resolution having been proposed and seconded by the aforementioned two Members, was put to the vote as a Special Resolution:

"RESOLVED THAT, subject to the provisions of the Securities Contracts (Regulation) Act, 1956, and the Securities and Exchange of Board of India, Act, 1992, and the rules framed thereunder and other applicable laws, rules and regulations and guidelines and subject to such other approvals, permission and sanctions as may be necessary and subject to such conditions as may be prescribed by The Securities and Exchange Board of India and Stock Exchanges while granting such approvals, permission and sanctions, which may be agreed to by the Board of Directors of the Company, which expression shall be deemed to include any Committee of the Board for the time powers conferred by the Board, the consent of the Company be and is hereby accorded to the Board to voluntarily de-list the equity shares of the Company from The Stock Exchange - Ahmedabad, The Calcutta Stock Exchange Association The Limited and Ludhiana Stock Exchange Association Limited.

"RESOLVED FURTHER THAT the Board be and is hereby authorised to do all acts, deeds and things as it may in its absolute discretion deem necessary and appropriate to give effect to the above Resolution."

On a show of hands, the Chairman declared the aforesaid Special Resolution carried with the requisite majority.

TERMINATION OF THE MEETING

The Meeting terminated with a vote of thanks to the Chair.

Secretarial Standard on General Meetings (SS-2)

Adherence by a company to this Secretarial Standard is mandatory, as per the provisions of the Companies Act, 2013.

INTRODUCTION

This Standard seeks to prescribe a set of principles for the convening and conducting of General Meetings and matters related thereto. This Standard also deals with conduct of e-voting and postal ballot.

SCOPE

This Standard is applicable to all types of General Meetings of all companies incorporated under the Act except One Person Company (OPC) and class or classes of companies which are exempted by the Central Government through notification. The principles enunciated in this Standard for General Meetings of Members are applicable mutatis mutand is to Meetings of debenture-holders and creditors. A Meeting of the Members or class of Members or debenture-holders or creditors of a company under the directions of the Court or the Company Law Board (CLB) or the National Company Law Tribunal (NCLT) or any other prescribed authority shall be governed by this Standard without prejudice to any rules, regulations and directions prescribed for and orders of, such courts, judicial forums and other authorities with respect to the conduct of such Meetings.

This Standard is in conformity with the provisions of the Act. However, if, due to subsequent changes in the Act, a particular Standard or any part thereof becomes inconsistent with the Act, the provisions of the Act shall prevail.

DEFINITIONS

The following terms are used in this Standard with the meaning specified:

"Act" means the Companies Act, 2013 (Act No. 18 of 2013) or any previous enactment thereof, or any statutory modification thereto or re-enactment thereof and includes any Rules and Regulations framed thereunder.

"Agency" means agency approved or recognised by the Ministry of Corporate Affairs and appointed by the Board for providing and supervising electronic platform for voting.

"Articles" means the Articles of Association of a company, as originally framed or as altered from time to time or applied in pursuance of any previous company law or the Companies Act, 2013.

"Calendar Year" means calendar year as per Gregorian calendar, i.e., a period of one year which begins on 1st January and ends on 31st December.

"Chairman" means the Chairman of the Board or the Chairman appointed or elected for a Meeting.

"Maintenance" means keeping registers and records either in physical or electronic form, as may be permitted under any law for the time being in force, and includes the making of necessary entries therein, the authentication of such entries and the preservation of such physical or electronic records.

"Meeting" or" General *Meeting"* or" Annual *General Meeting"* or" Extra-*Ordinary General Meeting"* means a duly convened, held and conducted Meeting of Members.

"Minutes" means a formal written record, in physical or electronic form, of the proceedings of a Meeting.

"Minutes Book" means a Book maintained in physical or in electronic form for the purpose of recording of Minutes.

"National Holiday" includes Republic Day, i.e., 26th January,

Independence Day, i.e., 15th August, Gandhi Jayanti, i.e., 2nd October and such other day as may be declared as National Holiday by the Central Government.

"Ordinary Business" means business to be transacted at an Annual general Meeting relating to (i) the consideration of financial statements, consolidated financial statements, if any, and the reports of the Board of Directors and Auditors; (ii) the declaration of any dividend; (iii) the appointment of Directors in the place of those retiring; and (iv) the appointment or ratification thereof and fixing of remuneration of the Auditors.

"Proxy" means an instrument in writing signed by a Member, authorising another person, whether a Member or not, to attend and vote on his behalf at a Meeting and also where the context so requires,the person so appointed by a Member.

"Quorum" means the minimum number of Members whose presenceis necessary for holding of a Meeting.

"Remote e-voting" means the facility of casting votes by a member using an electronic voting system from a place other than venue of a general meeting.

"Secretarial Auditor" means a Company Secretary in Practice appointed in pursuance of the Act to conduct the secretarial audit of the company.

"Secured Computer System" means computer hardware, software, and procedure that –

(a) are reasonably secure from unauthorized access and misuse;

(b) provide a reasonable level of reliability and correct operation;

(c) are reasonably suited to performing the intended functions;and

(d) adhere to generally accepted security procedures.

"Special Business" means business other than the Ordinary Business to be transacted at an Annual General Meeting and all business to be transacted at any other General Meeting. "Time stamp" means the current time of an event that is recorded by a Secured Computer System and is used to describe the time that is printed to a file or other location to help keep track of when data is added, removed, sent or received.

126

'Voting by electronic means, includes 'remote e-voting' and voting at the general meeting through an electronic voting system which maybe the same as used for remote e-voting. "Voting *by postal ballot"* means voting by ballot, by post or by electronic means.

"Voting Right" means the right of a Member to vote on any matter at a Meeting of Members or by means of e-voting or postal or physical ballot;

Words and expressions used and not defined herein shall have the meanings respectively assigned to them under the Act.

SECRETARIAL STANDARD

Features of the standard are reproduced as follows:

Meetings

A General Meeting shall be convened by or on the authority of the Board.

- Notice in writing of every Meeting shall be given to every Member of the company. Such Notice shall also be given to the Directors and Auditors of the Company, to the Secretarial Auditor, to Debenture Trustees, if any, and, wherever applicable or so required, to other specified persons.

- Notice shall be sent by hand or by ordinary post or by speed post or by registered post or by courier or by facsimile or by e-mail or by any other electronic means. 'Electronic means' means any communication sent by a company through its authorised and secured computer programme which is capable of producing confirmation and keeping record of such communication addressed to the person entitled to receive such communication at the last electronic mail address provided by the Member.

- In case of companies having a website, the Notices hall be hosted on the website.

- Notice shall specify the day, date, time and full address of the venue of the Meeting.

- Notice shall clearly specify the nature of the Meeting and the business to be transacted threat. In respect of items of Special Business, each such item shall be in the form of a Resolution and shall be accompanied by an explanatory statement which shall set out all such facts as would enable a Member to understand the meaning, scope and implications of the item of business and to take a decision thereon. In respect of items of Ordinary Business, Resolutions are not required to be stated in the Notice except where the Auditors or Directors to be appointed are other than the retiring Auditors or Directors, as the case may be.

- Notice and accompanying documents shall be given at least twenty-one clear days in advance of the Meeting.

- Notice and accompanying documents may be given at a shorter period of time if consent in writing is given thereto, by physical or electronic means, by not less than ninety-five per cent of the Members entitled to vote at such Meeting.

- No business shall be transacted at a Meeting if Notice in accordance with this Standard has not been given.

- No items of business other than those specified in the Notice and those specifically permitted under the Act shall be taken up at the Meeting.

- Notice shall be accompanied, by an attendance slip and a Proxy form with clear instructions for filling, stamping, signing and/or depositing the Proxy form.

- A Meeting convened upon due Notice shall not be postponed or cancelled.

Frequency

Frequency of Meetings.

129

- Every company shall, in each Calendar Year, hold a General Meeting called the Annual General Meeting.

- Extra-Ordinary General Meeting. Items of business other than Ordinary Business may be considered at an Extra-Ordinary General Meeting or by means of a postal ballot, if thought fit by the Board.

QUORUM

- Quorum shall be present throughout the Meeting.

- A duly authorised representative of a body corporate or the representative of the President of India or the Governor of a State is deemed to be a Member personally present and enjoys all the rights of a Member present in person.

Directors and Auditors

- If any Director is unable to attend the Meeting, the Chairman shall explain such absence at the Meeting.

- Directors who attend General Meetings of the Company and the Company Secretary shall be seated with the Chairman. The Company Secretary shall assist the Chairman in conducting the Meeting.

- The Auditors, unless exempted by the company, shall, either by themselves or through their authorised representative, attend the General Meetings of the company and shall have the right to be heard at such Meetings on that part of the business which concerns them as Auditors. The authorised representative who attends the General Meeting of the Company shall also be qualified to be an Auditor.

- The Secretarial Auditor, unless exempted by the company shall, either by himself or through his authorised representative, attend the Annual General Meeting and shall have the right to be heard at such Meeting on that part of the business which concerns him as Secretarial Auditor.

Chairman

- The Chairman of the Board shall take the chair and conduct the Meeting. If the Chairman is not present within fifteen minutes after the time appointed for holding the Meeting, or if he is unwilling to act as Chairman of the Meeting, or if no Director has been so designated, the Directors present at the Meeting shall elect one of themselves to be the Chairman of the Meeting. If no Director is present within fifteen minutes after the time appointed for holding the Meeting, or if no Director is willing to take the chair, the Members present shall elect, on a show of hands, one of themselves to be the Chairman of the Meeting, unless otherwise provided in the Articles.

- The Chairman shall explain the objective and implications of the Resolutions before they are put to vote at the Meeting.

- In case of public companies, the Chairman shall not propose any Resolution in which he is deemed to be concerned or interested nor shall he conduct the proceedings for that item of business.

Proxies

- A Member entitled to attend and vote is entitled to appoint a Proxy, or where that is allowed, one or more proxies, to attend and vote instead of himself and a Proxy need not be a Member.

- An instrument appointing a Proxy shall be either in the Form specified in the Articles or in the Form set out in the Act.

- An instrument of Proxy duly filled, stamped and signed, is valid only for the Meeting to which it relates including any adjournment thereof.

- An instrument of Proxy is valid only if it is properly stamped as per the applicable law. Unstamped or inadequately stamped Proxies or Proxies upon which the stamps have not been cancelled are invalid.

- The Proxy-holder shall prove his identity at the time of attending the Meeting.

- An authorised representative of a body corporate or of the President of India or of the Governor of a State, holding shares in a company, may appoint a Proxy under his signature.

Proxies in Blank and Incomplete Proxies

- A Proxy form which does not state the name of the Proxy shall not be considered valid.

- Undated Proxy shall not be considered valid.

- If a company receives multiple Proxies for the same holdings of a Member, the Proxy which is dated last shall be considered valid; if they are not dated or bear the same date without specific mention of time, all such multiple Proxies shall be treated as invalid.

Deposit of Proxies

- Proxies shall be deposited with the company either in person or through post not later than forty-eight hours before the commencement of the Meeting in relation to which they are deposited and a Proxy shall be accepted even on a holiday if the last date by which it could be accepted is a holiday.

133

- If the Articles so provide, a Member who has not appointed a Proxy to attend and vote on his behalf at a Meeting may appoint a Proxy for any adjourned Meeting, not later than forty-eight hours before the time of such adjourned Meeting.

- If a Proxy had been appointed for the original Meeting and such Meeting is adjourned, any Proxy given for the adjourned Meeting revokes the Proxy given for the original Meeting.

- A Proxy later in date revokes any Proxy/Proxies dated prior to such Proxy.

- A Proxy is valid until written notice of revocation has been received by the company before the commencement of the Meeting or adjourned Meeting, as the case may be.

- When a Member appoints a Proxy and both the Member and Proxy attend the Meeting, the Proxy stands automatically revoked.

Inspection of Proxies

- Requisitions, if any, for inspection of Proxies shall be received in writing from a Member entitled to vote on any Resolution at least three days before the commencement of the Meeting.

- Proxies shall be made available for inspection during the period beginning twenty-four hours before the time fixed for the commencement of the Meeting and ending with the conclusion of the Meeting. Inspection shall be allowed between 9 a.m. and 6 p.m. during such period.

- A fresh requisition, conforming to the above requirements, shall be given for inspection of Proxies in case the original Meeting is adjourned.

- All Proxies received by the company shall be recorded chronologically in a register kept for that purpose.

- In case any Proxy entered in the register is rejected, the reasons there for shall be entered in the remarks column.

Voting

- Every Resolution shall be proposed by a Member and seconded by another Member.

- Every company having its equity shares listed on a recognized stock exchange other than companies whose equity shares are listed on SME Exchange or on the Institutional Trading Platform and other companies as prescribed shall provide e-voting facility to their Members to exercise their Voting Rights.

- Every company, which has provided e-voting facility to its Members, shall also put every Resolution to vote through a ballot process at the Meeting.

- Every company shall, at the meeting, put every resolution, except a resolution which has been put to Remote e-voting, to vote on a show of hands at the first instance, unless a poll is validly demanded.

- Proxy cannot vote on a show of hands.

- The Chairman shall order a poll upon receipt of a valid demand for poll either before or on the declaration of the result of the voting on any Resolution on show of hands.

- Every member holding equity shares and, in certain cases as prescribed in the Act, every Member holding preference shares, shall be entitled to vote on a Resolution.

- A Member who is a related party is not entitled to vote on a Resolution relating to approval of any contract or arrangement in which such Member is a related party.

- Unless otherwise provided in the Articles, in the event of equality of votes, whether on show of hands or electronically or on a poll, the Chairman of the Meeting shall have a second or casting vote.

- Every company that is required or opts to provide e-voting facility to its Members shall comply with the provisions in this regard.

- Every company providing e-voting facility shall offer such facility to all Members, irrespective of whether they hold shares in physical form or in dematerialised form.

- The facility for Remote e-voting shall remain open for not less than three days. The voting period shall close at 5 p.m. on the day preceding the date of the General Meeting.

Board Approval. The Board shall appoint one or more scrutinisers for e-voting or the ballot process,

- appoint an Agency;

- decide the cut-off date for the purpose of reckoning the names of Members who are entitled to Voting Rights;

- authorise the Chairman or in his absence, any other Director to receive the scrutiniser's register, report on e-voting and other related papers with requisite details.

Notice of the Meeting, wherein the facility of e voting is provided, shall be sent either by registered post or speed post or by courier or by e-mail or by any other electronic means.

- Notice shall also be placed on the website of the Company, in case of companies having a website, and of the Agency.

- Such Notice shall remain on the website till the date of General Meeting.

- Notice shall inform the Members about procedure of Remote e-voting, availability of such facility and provide necessary information thereof to enable them to access such facility.

- Based on the scrutiniser's report received on Remotee-voting and voting at the Meeting, the Chairman or any other Director so authorised shall countersign the scrutiniser's report and declare the result of the voting forthwith with details of the number of votes cast for and against the Resolution, invalid votes and whether the Resolution has been carried or not.

- The result of the voting, with details of the number of votes cast for and against the Resolution, invalid votes and whether the Resolution has been carried or not shall be displayed on the Notice Board of the company at its Registered Office and its Head Office as well as Corporate Office, if any, if such office is situated elsewhere. Further, the results of voting alongwith the scrutiniser's report shall also be placed on the website of the company, in case of companies having a website and of the Agency, immediately after the results are declared.

The Resolution, if passed by a requisite majority, shall be deemed to have been passed on the date of the relevant General Meeting.

Custody of scrutinisers' register, report and other related papers The scrutinisers' register, report and other related papers received from the scrutiniser(s) shall be kept in the custody of the Company Secretary or any other person authorised by the Board for this purpose.

Conduct of Poll

- When a poll is demanded on any Resolution, the Chairman shall get the validity of the demand verified and, if the demand is valid, shall order the poll forthwith if it is demanded on the question of appointment of the Chairman or adjournment of the Meeting and, in any other case, within forty-eight hours of the demand for poll.

- In the case of a poll, which is not taken forthwith, the Chairman shall announce the date, venue and time of taking the poll to enable Members to have adequate and convenient opportunity to exercise their vote. The Chairman may permit any Member who so desires to be present at the time of counting of votes.

- Each Resolution put to vote by poll shall be put to vote separately. One ballot paper may be used for more than one item.

- The Chairman shall appoint such number of scrutinisers, as he deems necessary, who may include a Company Secretary in Practice, a Chartered Accountant in Practice, a Cost Accountant in Practice, an Advocate or any other person of repute who is not in the employment of the Company, to ensure that the scrutiny of the votes cast on a poll is done in a fair and transparent manner.

- Based on the scrutiniser's report, the Chairman shall declare the result of the poll within two days of the submission of report by the scrutiniser, with details of the number of votes cast for and against the Resolution, invalid votes and whether the Resolution has been carried or not.

- The result of the poll with details of the number of votes cast for and against the Resolution, invalid votes and whether the Resolution has been carried or not shall be displayed on the Notice Board of the company at its Registered Office and its Head Office as well as Corporate Office, if any, if such office is situated elsewhere, and in case of companies having a website, shall also be placed on the website.

- The result of the poll shall be deemed to be the decision of the Meeting on the Resolution on which the poll was taken.

- Resolutions for items of business which are likely to affect the market price of the securities of the company shall not be withdrawn. However, any resolution proposed for consideration through e-voting shall not be withdrawn.

- A Resolution passed at a Meeting shall not be rescinded otherwise than by a Resolution passed at a subsequent Meeting.

- Modifications to any Resolution which do not change the purpose of the Resolution materially may be proposed, seconded and adopted by the requisite majority at the Meeting and, thereafter, the modified Resolution shall be duly proposed, seconded and put to vote.

- The qualifications, observations or comments or other remarks on the financial transactions or matters which have any adverse effect on the functioning of the company, if any, mentioned in the Auditor's Report shall be read at the Annual General Meeting and attention of the Members present shall be drawn to the explanations / comments given by the Board of Directors in their report.

- The qualifications, observations or comments or other remarks if any, mentioned in the Secretarial Audit Report issued by the Company Secretary in Practice, shall be read at the Annual General Meeting and attention of Members present shall be drawn to the explanations/ comments given by the Board of Directors in their report.

- No gifts, gift coupons, or cash in lieu of gifts shall be distributed to Members at or in connection with the Meeting.

- A duly convened Meeting shall not be adjourned unless circumstances so warrant. The Chairman may adjourn a Meeting with the consent of the Members, at which a Quorum is present, and shall adjourn a Meeting if so directed by the Members.

- If a Meeting is adjourned *sine-die* or for a period of thirty days or more, a Notice of the adjourned Meeting shall be given in accordance with the provisions contained herein above relating to Notice.

- If a Meeting is adjourned for a period of less than thirty days, the company shall give not less than three days' Notice specifying the day, date, time and venue of the Meeting, to the Members either individually or by publishing an advertisement in a vernacular newspaper in the principal vernacular language of the district in which the registered office of the company is situated, and in an

English newspaper in English language, both having a wide circulation in that district.

- If a Meeting, other than a requisitioned Meeting, stands adjourned for want of Quorum, the adjourned Meeting shall be held on the same day, in the next week at the same time and place or on such other day, not being a National Holiday, or at such other time and place as may be determined by the Board.

- If, within half an hour from the time appointed for holding a Meeting called by requisitionists, a Quorum is not present, the Meeting shall stand cancelled.

- At an adjourned Meeting, only the unfinished business of the original Meeting shall be considered. Any Resolution passed at an adjourned Meeting would be deemed to have been passed on the date of the adjourned Meeting and not on any earlier date.

Passing of Resolutions by postal ballot

- Every company, except a company having less than or equal to two hundred Members, shall transact items of business as prescribed, only by means of postal ballot instead of transacting such business at a General Meeting.

- Every company having its equity shares listed on a recognized stock exchange other than companies whose equity shares are listed on SME Exchange or on the Institutional Trading Platform and other companies which are required to provide e-voting facility shall provide such facility to its Members in respect of those items, which are required to be transacted through postal ballot.

- Notice of the postal ballot shall be given in writing to every Member of the company. Such Notice shall be sent either by registered post or speed post, or by courier or by e-mail or by any other electronic means at the address registered with the company.

- In case of companies having a website, Notice of the postal ballot shall also be placed on the website.

- Notice shall specify the day, date, time and venue where the results of the voting by postal ballot will be announced and the link of the website where such results will be displayed.

- Notice of the postal ballot shall inform the Members about availability of e-voting facility, if any, and provide necessary information thereof to enable them to access such facility.

- Each item proposed to be passed through postal ballot shall be in the form of a Resolution and shall be accompanied by

144

an explanatory statement which shall set out all such facts as would enable a Member to understand the meaning, scope and implications of the item of business and to take a decision thereon.

- The postal ballot form shall be accompanied by a postage prepaid reply envelope addressed to the scrutiniser. A single postal ballot Form may provide for multiple items of business to be transacted.

- The postal ballot form shall contain instructions as to the manner in which the form is to be completed, assent or dissent is to be recorded and its return to the scrutiniser. The postal ballot form may specify instances in which such Form shall be treated as invalid or rejected and procedure for issue of duplicate postal ballot Forms.

- A postal ballot form shall be considered invalid if:

- A form other than one issued by the company has been used;

- It has not been signed by or on behalf of the Member;

- Signature on the postal ballot form doesn't match the specimen signatures with the company

- It is not possible to determine without any doubt the assent or dissent of the Member;

- Neither assent nor dissent is mentioned;

- Any competent authority has given directions in writing to the company to freeze the Voting Rights of the Member;

- The envelope containing the postal ballot form is received after the last date prescribed;

- The postal ballot form, signed in a representative capacity, is not accompanied by a certified copy of the relevant specific authority;

- It is received from a Member who is in arrears of payment of calls;

- It is defaced or mutilated in such a way that its identity as a genuine form cannot be established

- Member has made any amendment to the Resolution or imposed any condition while exercising his vote.

- Based on the scrutiniser's report, the Chairman or any other Director authorised by him shall declare the result of the postal ballot on the date, time and venue specified in the Notice, with details of the number of votes cast for and against the Resolution, invalid votes and the final result as to whether the Resolution has been carried or not.

- The result of the voting with details of the number of votes cast for and against the Resolution, invalid votes and whether the Resolution has been carried or not, along with the scrutiniser's report shall be displayed on the Notice Board of the company at its Registered Office and its Head Office as well as Corporate Office, if any, if such office is situated elsewhere, and also be placed on the website of the company, in case of companies having a website.

- The Resolution, if passed by requisite majority, shall be deemed to have been passed on the last date specified by the company for receipt of duly completed postal ballot forms or e-voting. Custody of scrutiniser's registers, report and other related papers The postal ballot forms, other related papers, register and scrutiniser's report received from the scrutiniser shall be kept in the custody of the Company Secretary or any other person authorised by the Board for this purpose.

- A Resolution passed by postal ballot shall not be rescinded otherwise than by a Resolution passed subsequently through postal ballot.

- No amendment or modification shall be made to any Resolution circulated to the Members for passing by means of postal ballot.

147

Minutes

- Every company shall keep Minutes of all Meetings. Minutes kept in accordance with the provisions of the Act evidence the proceedings recorded therein. Minutes help in understanding the deliberations and decisions taken at the Meeting.

- A distinct Minutes Book shall be maintained for Meetings of the Members of the company, creditors and others as may be required under the Act. Resolutions passed by postal ballot shall be recorded in the Minutes book of General Meetings.

- Minutes may be maintained in electronic form in such manner as prescribed under the Act and as may be decided by the Board. Minutes in electronic form shall be maintained with Time stamp.

- The pages of the Minutes Books shall be consecutively numbered.

- Minutes shall not be pasted or attached to the Minutes Book, or tampered with in any manner.

- Minutes of Meetings, if maintained in loose-leaf form, shall be bound periodically depending on the size and volume. There shall be a proper locking device to ensure security and proper control to prevent removal or manipulation of the loose leaves.

- Minutes Books shall be kept at the Registered office of the company or at such other place, as may be approved by the Board.

- Minutes shall state, at the beginning the Meeting, name of the company, day, date,venue and time of commencement and conclusion of the Meeting.

- Minutes shall record the names of the Directors and the Company Secretary present at the Meeting.The names of the Directors shall be listed in alphabetical order or in any other logical manner, but in either case starting with the name of the person in the Chair.

- Minutes shall, *inter alia*, contain:

  o The Record of election, if any, of the Chairman of the Meeting.

  o The fact that certain registers, documents,the Auditor's Report and Secretarial Audit

  o Report, as prescribed under the Act were available for inspection.

  o The Record of presence of Quorum.

o The number of Members present in person including representatives.

o The number of proxies and the number of shares represented by them.

o The presence of the Chairmen of the Audit Committee, Nomination and Remuneration Committee and Stakeholders Relationship Committee or their authorised representatives.

o The presence if any, of the Secretarial Auditor, the Auditors, or their authorised representatives, the Court/Tribunal appointed observers or scrutinisers.

o Summary of the opening remarks of the Chairman.

o Reading of qualifications, observations or comments or other remarks on the financial transactions or matters which have any adverse effect on the functioning of the Company, as mentioned in the report of the Auditors.

o Reading of qualifications, observations or comments or other remarks as mentioned in the report of the Secretarial Auditor.

o Summary of the clarifications provided on various Agenda Items.

- In respect of each Resolution, the type of the Resolution, the names of the persons who proposed and seconded and the majority with which such Resolution was passed.

- In the case of poll, the names of scrutinisers appointed and the number of votes cast in favour and against the Resolution and invalid votes.

- If the Chairman vacates the Chair in respect of any specific item, the fact that he did so and in his place some other Director or Member took the Chair.

- The time of commencement and conclusion of the Meeting.

- In respect of Resolutions passed by e-voting or postal ballot, a brief report on the e-voting or postal ballot conducted including the Resolution proposed, the result of the voting thereon and the summary of the scrutiniser's report shall be recorded in the Minutes Book and signed by the Chairman or in the event of death or inability of the Chairman, by any Director duly authorised by the Board for the purpose, within thirty days from the date of passing of Resolution by e-voting or postal ballot.

- Minutes shall contain a fair and correct summary of the proceedings of the Meeting.

151

- Minutes shall be written in clear, concise and plain language. Minutes shall be written in third person and past tense. Resolutions shall however be written in present tense.Minutes need not be an exact transcript of the proceedings at the Meeting.

- Each item of business taken up at the Meeting shall be numbered. Numbering shall be in a manner which would enable ease of reference or cross-reference.

- Minutes shall be entered in the Minutes Book within thirty days from the date of conclusion of the Meeting.

- The date of entry of the Minutes in the Minutes book shall be recorded by the Company Secretary.

- Minutes, once entered in the Minutes Book, shall not be altered.

- Minutes of a General Meeting shall be signed and dated by the Chairman of the Meeting or in the event of death or inability of that Chairman, by any Director who was present in the Meeting and duly authorised by the Board for the purpose, within thirty days of the General Meeting.

- The Chairman shall initial each page of the Minutes, sign the last page and append to such signature the date on which and the place where he has signed the Minutes.

- Directors and Members are entitled to inspect the Minutes of all General Meetings including Resolutions passed by postal ballot.

- Extract of the Minutes shall be given only after the Minutes have been duly signed. However, any Resolution passed at a Meeting may be issued even pending signing of the Minutes, provided the same is certified by the Chairman or any Director or the Company Secretary.

- Minutes of all Meetings shall be preserved permanently in physical or in electronic form with Time stamp.

- Office copies of Notices, scrutiniser's report, and related papers shall be preserved in good order in physical or in electronic form for as long as they remain current or for eight financial years, whichever is later and may be destroyed thereafter with the approval of the Board.

- Minutes Books shall be kept in the custody of the Company Secretary. Where there is no Company Secretary, Minutes shall be kept in the custody of any Director duly authorised for the purpose by the Board.

Annual Report

- Every listed company shall prepare a report on Annual General Meeting in the prescribed form, including a

153

confirmation that the Meeting was convened, held and conducted as per the provisions of the Act.

- The Annual Return of a company shall disclose the date of Annual general Meeting held during the financial year.

EFFECTIVE DATE

This Standard has come into effect from 1st July, 2015

CHAPTER 4

Meetings of Directors

Board Meetings (Section 173 of Companies Act, 2013)

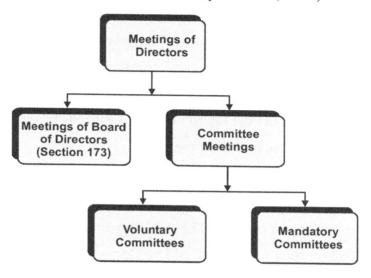

According to section 2 (10) of the Companies Act, 2013, "Board of Directors" or "Board", in relation to a company, means the collective body of the directors of the company. The Board of Directors is the top most decision making body of a company. It is saddled with wide powers and responsibilities. The business of the Board is conducted through meetings. The Board meetings are very significant because all the major decisions of the company are taken in the Board meetings. Although important business is also transacted in AGMs or EGMs but such meetings are more formal in nature and their course of direction is generally delineated by the Board and the decisions that are taken in these meetings are predictable.

Regulation 67 (1) of Table F provides that the Board of Directors may meet for the dispatch of business, adjourn and otherwise regulate its meetings, as it thinks fit. This provision indicates that as a general rule the directors must exercise their powers collectively as Board. Thus they should as a rule exercise their powers in duly convened meetings but the Board may take decisions by resolutions passed by circulation, instead of meetings.

Frequency of Board meetings

- According to section 173 (1) every company shall hold the first meeting of its Board of Directors within 30 days of the date of incorporation.

- Thereafter, it shall hold a minimum of four such meetings every year in such a manner that not more than 120 days shall intervene between two consecutive meetings.

- As per clause 49 of the listing agreement (SEBI), every listed company, which is covered by this clause, is, required to hold at least four Board meetings in a year with a maximum time gap of four months between any two meetings.

- Further, in case of a Section 8 company (not for profit companies) a board meeting should be held once in every six months.

- However the Central Government is empowered to relax this rule with regard to any class of companies.

Notice of Board

MeetingLength of notice and means of communication. A meeting of the Board shall be called by giving not less than 7 days' notice in writing to every director at his address registered with the company and such notice shall be sent by hand delivery or by post or by electronic means. {Section 173(3) of Companies Act, 2013}.

Shorter notice.

The Board Meeting can be called by giving a shorter notice in writing provided at least one independent director, if any, is present in the meeting. If however, an independent director is not present the decisions taken at such meeting should be circulated to all director and shall be final only on ratification by at least one independent director, if any.

Notice to every director is compulsory.

It is compulsory for the company to send notice of the meeting to every director at his registered address even if a director has expressed his inability to attend the meeting. According to Section 173 (4), every officer of the company whose duty is to give notice under this section and who fails to do so shall be liable to penalty of ` 25,000.

Notice to a director will be exempted in the following cases:

- Where notice is not given as required, but all directors attend the meeting and do not object to the absence of notice, or
- Where the director who is absent does not complain and ratifies the proceedings in a subsequent meeting where he is present.

Form of notice. The form of notice has not been specified in the Act. But it should ordinarily specify the date, day, time and full address and venue of the meeting. The notice should inform the directors if the facility of participation through Electronic Mode is available.

Notice to Sock Exchange. Listed companies are required to provide a notice of the Board Meeting to the Sock Exchange/s where the securities of the company are listed under clause 49 of the listing agreement with the stock exchange/s.

Place and time of Meeting

The Act does not specify any place of meeting of the Board. Thus a Board Meeting can be held anywhere at the convenience of the directors. In other words it is not compulsory for the company to

hold the Board meeting at the registered office or in the city where the registered office is situated.

Quorum

- According to Section 174 the quorum of a Board Meeting should be $1/3^{rd}$ of the total strength of or two directors, whichever is higher. The participation of directors through video conferencing or by other audio means will also be counted for the purpose of quorum.

- If there is a vacancy in the Board of Directors the remaining Directors can continue to hold Board meetings as usual, but if as a result of vacancy the number of directors falls below the quorum fixed under the Act, the remaining directors can proceed to increase the number of directors to the strength required for quorum. They can call a general meeting only for this purpose.

- Where at any time the number of interested directors exceeds or is equal to $2/3^{rd}$ of the total strength of the Board of Directors, the number of directors who are not interested directors and present at the meeting, being not less than two, shall be the quorum during such time.

- Where a meeting of the Board could not be held for want of quorum, then, unless the articles of the company otherwise provide, the meeting shall automatically stand adjourned to the same day at the same time and place in the next week or

159

if that day is a national holiday, till the next succeeding day, which is not a national holiday, at the same time and place.

- While counting quorum

    o any fraction of a number shall be rounded off as one;

    o total strength" shall not include directors whose places are vacant.

- According to the Secretarial Standards on Meetings of Board of Directors, The quorum should be present throughout the meeting.

Agenda

The Companies Act does not stipulate that the agenda or the business to be transacted at the Board Meeting should be mentioned in the notice. But according to convention the notice usually contains the agenda of the meeting. The agenda can be written in the notice itself or may be attached to the notice.

Chairman

- The office of the chairman is a prerequisite to make a Board meeting valid.

- Usually the Articles of Association of the company provide regulations regarding the appointment of chairman.

- If the articles are silent about the manner of the appointment of chairman, the directors themselves may elect the chairman and fix his term office at the first meeting or in any subsequent meeting as is necessary.

- If the chairman is absent from a meeting till five minutes from the commencement of the meeting, the directors can proceed with the meeting by appointing a new director from among the directors present.

- The chairman is an important official who is saddled with the responsibility of conducting the Board meeting according to the requirements of law and that the meeting is conducted in an orderly manner.. He has to also ensure that minutes are kept properly.

Resolution by Circulation

The decisions relating to the company are taken by the Board of directors in their meetings. Such meetings are required to be held at regular intervals as specified in the Act. But it may not be practically possible to hold such meetings when decisions are required urgently. The Rule 5 of the Companies (meeting of Board and Power) Rules 2014, prescribe that a resolution may be circulated to the directors together with the necessary papers for seeking their approval which may include E-mail or Fax.

Procedure for passing a board resolution by circulation:

1.   The draft of the resolution should be sent to all the directors.

2.   If all or a majority of the directors entitled to vote on the resolution approve the resolution, the resolution will be deemed to have been carried.

3.   The resolution should be recorded in the minutes of the immediately next Board Meeting.

4.   The circular resolution should be enclosed in the notice for the immediately next Board Meeting along with details of how many directors voted in favour and how many dissented.

Voting at Board Meetings

Directors usually take recourse to voting by show of hands to carry resolutions in Board Meetings. However a poll may be demanded, but the usual method of voting is show of hands. In Board Meetings proxy voting is not allowed. The principle of 'one man one vote' is followed in Board Meetings. However, usually the chairman holds a casting vote. Where a director has an 'interest' (as per Section 184), he will not be entitled to vote but has a right to attend the meeting.

Minutes of Board Meeting

The Board Meetings should be recorded in a separate minutes book. Minutes of each Board meeting should be recorded in 30 days from the conclusion of the meeting. In addition to the usual issues, according to Section 118 (2) of the Companies Act, 2013, in the case of a meeting of the Board of Directors or of a committee of the Board, the Minutes shall also contain—

(*a*)   the names of the directors present at the meeting; and

(*b*)   in the case of each resolution passed at the meeting and

(c)   the names of the directors if any, dissenting from, or not concurring with the resolution.

Meetings of Committees

Voluntary Committees/ Under Articles of Association

Since the Board cannot meet as often, as required, it is a common practice in companies, if permitted by Articles of Association, to delegate the work of decision making to committees of Directors. Such committees may have as less as one member if the articles do not prohibit.

The rules contained under Regulation 71-75 of Table F to Schedule 1 may be followed for the composition and conduct of committee meetings.

1.   The Board may, subject to the provisions of the Act, delegate any of its powers to committees consisting of such member or members of its body as it thinks fit;

2. Any committee so formed shall in the exercise of the powers so delegated, conform to any regulations that may be imposed on it by the Board.

3. A committee may elect a chairman of its meetings,

4. If no such chairman is elected, or if at any meeting the chairman is not present within five minutes after the time appointed for holding the meeting, the members present may choose one of their member to be chairman of the meeting."

5. A committee may meet and adjourn as it thinks proper

6. Questions arising at any meeting of a committee shall be determined by a majority of votes of the members present and in case of an equality of votes, the chairman shall have a second or casting vote.

7. A resolution in writing by all the members of the Committee or Board shall be valid and effectual as if it had been passed at a meeting of the Board or Committee duly convened.

Mandatory committees under Companies Act, 2013

The Companies Act, 2013 provides for constitution of some committees. According to this Act the following committees are to be formed by a company-

☐ Audit Committee under Section 177,

☐ Nomination and Remuneration Committee under Section 178(1),

☐ Stakeholders Relationship Committee under Section 178(5) and

☐ Corporate and Social Responsibility Committee under Section 135.

1. Audit Committee

It is necessary for the following kinds of companies to constitute an audit committee:

(i) Every Listed Company,

(ii) Every public company having a paid up capital of ` ten crore or more,

(iii) Every public company having turnover of ` one hundred crore or more,

(iv) Every company which have in aggregate outstanding loan or borrowing or debentures or deposits exceeding ` Fifty crore rupees.

Composition. The Audit Committee shall consist of a minimum of three directors with independent directors forming a majority. The majority of members of Audit Committee including its Chairperson shall be persons with ability to read and understand, the financial statement.

Terms of reference. Every Audit Committee shall act in accordance with the terms of reference specified in writing by the Board which shall, include the following matters—

(*i*)   The recommendation for appointment, remuneration and terms of appointment of auditors of the company;

(*ii*)   Review and monitor the auditor's independence and performance, and effectiveness of audit process;

(*iii*)   Examination of the financial statement and the auditors' report thereon;

(*iv*)   Approval or any subsequent modification of transactions of the company with related parties;

(*v*)   Scrutiny of inter-corporate loans and investments;

(*vi*)   Valuation of undertakings or assets of the company, wherever it is necessary;

(*vii*)   Evaluation of internal financial controls and risk management systems;

(*viii*) Monitoring the end use of funds raised through public offers and related matters.

166

Discussions with statutory and internal auditors. The Audit Committee may call for the comments of the auditors about internal control systems, the scope of audit, including the observations of the auditors and review of financial statement before their submission to the Board and may also discuss any related issues with the internal and statutory auditors and the management of the company.

Power to investigate. The Audit Committee shall have authority to investigate into any matter in relation to the items specified in sub-section (4) or referred to it by the Board and for this purpose shall have power to obtain professional advice from external sources and have full access to information contained in the records of the company.

Recommendations of Audit Committee. The recommendations of the audit committee are binding for the Board. Where the Board does not accept any recommendations it will be required to record the reasons in the Annual Report.

Penalty. Where default is made by the company in complying with the provisions of section 177, the company shall be punishable with fine which shall not be less than? one lakh but which may extend to ` five lakh and every officer of the company who is in default shall be punishable with imprisonment for a term which may extend to one year or with fine which shall not be less than ` twenty-five thousand but which may extend to ` one lakh rupees, or with both.

2. Nomination and Remuneration Committee and Stakeholders Relationship Committee (Section 178)

The Board of Directors of every listed company and such other class or classes of companies, as may be prescribed shall constitute the Nomination and Remuneration Committee

Composition. The committee should consist of three or more non-executive directors out of which not less than one-half shall be independent directors. The chairman of the company ny (whether executive or non-executive) may be appointed as a member of the Nomination and Remuneration Committee but shall not chair such Committee.

Job of the committee. The Nomination and Remuneration Committee shall identify persons who are qualified to become directors and who may be appointed in senior management in accordance with the criteria laid down, recommend to the Board their appointment and removal and shall carry out evaluation of every director's performance.The Nomination and Remuneration Committee shall formulate the criteria for determining qualifications, positive attributes and independence of a director and recommend to the Board a policy, relating to the remuneration for the directors, key managerial personnel and other employees.

The Nomination and Remuneration Committee shall, while formulating the policy under sub-section (3) ensure that—

(*a*)   the level and composition of remuneration is reasonable and sufficient to attract, retain and motivate directors of the quality required to run the company successfully;

(*b*)   relationship of remuneration to performance is clear and meets appropriate performance benchmarks; and

(*c*)   remuneration to directors, key managerial personnel and senior management involves a balance between fixed and incentive pay reflecting short and long-term performance objectives appropriate to the working of the company and its goals. Provided that such policy shall be disclosed in the Board's report.

3. Stakeholders' relationship committee

Requirement. The Board of Directors of a company which consists of more than one thousand shareholders, debenture-holders, deposit-holders and any other security holders at any time during a financial year shall constitute a Stakeholders Relationship Committee.

Composition. The committee shall consist of a chairperson who shall be a non-executive director and such other members as may be decided by the Board.

Job of the committee. The Stakeholders Relationship Committee shall consider and resolve the grievances of security holders of the company.

The chairperson of each of the committees constituted under this section or, in his absence, any other member of the committee authorised by him in this behalf shall attend the general meetings of the company.

Penalty. In case of any contravention of the provisions of section 177 and this section, the Company shall be punishable with fine which shall not be less than ` one lakh but which may extend to ` five lakh and every officer of the company who is in default shall be punishable with imprisonment for a term which may extend to one year or with fine which shall not be less than ` twenty-five thousand but which may extend to ` one lakh, or with both.

4. Corporate Social Responsibility Committee

Requirement. Every company having net worth of rupees five hundred crore or more, or turnover of rupees one thousand crore or more or a net profit of rupees five crore or more during any financial year shall constitute a Corporate Social Responsibility Committee.

Composition. The committee shall consist of three or more directors, out of which at least one director shall be an independent director.

Reporting. The Board's report under sub-section (*3*) of section 134 shall disclose the composition of the Corporate Social Responsibility Committee.

Job of the committee. The Corporate Social Responsibility Committee shall:

(*a*)   formulate and recommend to the Board, a Corporate Social Responsibility Policy which shall indicate the activities to be undertaken by the company as specified in Schedule VII;

(*b*)   recommend the amount of expenditure to be incurred on the activities referred to in clause (*a*); and

(*c*)   monitor the Corporate Social Responsibility Policy of the company from time to time.

Duty of the Board. The Board of every company referred to in sub-section
(*1*) shall,—

(*a*)   after taking into account the recommendations made by the Corporate Social Responsibility Committee, approve the Corporate Social Responsibility Policy for the Company and disclose contents of such Policy in its report and also place it on the Company's website, if any, in such manner as may be prescribed; and

(*b*)   ensure that the activities as are included in Corporate Social Responsibility Policy of the company are undertaken by the company.

Quantum of Spending. The Board of every company referred to in sub-section (*1*), shall ensure that the company spends, in every financial year, at least two per cent. of the average net profits of the company made during the three immediately preceding financial years, in pursuance of its Corporate Social Responsibility Policy: provided that the company shall give preference to the local area and areas around it where it operates, for spending the amount earmarked for Corporate Social Responsibility activities. Provided further that if the company fails to spend such amount, the Board shall, in its report made under clause (*o*) of sub-section (*3*) of section 134, specify the reasons for not spending the amount.

Duties of Company Secretary relating to Board Meetings (SS-1)

Before the meeting

1.   The Secretary has to ensure that the Board Meetings are held within the specified time frame. He has to specifically ensure that:

(a)   The first meeting of the Board is being held within 30 days,

(b)   That a minimum of four meetings of the Board are held every year and

(c)   That not more than 120 days intervene between two consecutive meetings.

172

(d)   In case of listed companies, at least four Board meetings are held in a year and the time gap between two meetings should not be more than four months.

2.   The Secretary has to ensure that the notice for the Board meeting is served on every director at least 7 days before the proposed meeting. He may choose to get it delivered by hand, post or electronically.

3.   Contact and request all the directors to attend the meeting and arrange the facilities required by them in this regard, like conveyance, stay arrangements, location of venue etc.

4.   The Secretary in consultation with the chairman should draft the agenda and arrange to send it to the directors.

5.   He should make available to the directors all documents, explanations, agreements, correspondence etc. in connection with the agenda.

6.   In case of first meeting the following documents should be ready:

(i)   Original certificate of Incorporation.

(ii)   Copy of Memorandum and Articles of Association.

(iii)   Copies of Form Nos. INC-1 (Application for reservation of name), INC-7 (Application for Incorporation),INC-11 (Application of Incorporation), INC-21 (Declaration prior to the commencement of business or exercising borrowing), INC-22 (Notice of situation of Registered Office) and power of attorney.

(iv)   Consent of directors;

(v)   Design etc. of common seal, share certificate, sign board, name plate, letterhead etc.

(vi)   Statement of preliminary expenses incurred.

(vii)   Certificate in writing about eligibility to appointment from the proposed Auditors [Second and third proviso to Section 139(1)].

(viii)   Certificate in writing about eligibility to appointment from the proposed Secretarial Auditor.

(ix)   Account opening form of the Bank with which Bank account of the company is to be opened.

(x)   Cheques/drafts from members towards payment for the shares agreed to be taken by them.

(xi)   Application(s) of qualified secretary to be appointed as secretary.

(xii)   Original/copies of agreement entered into between the promoters before the incorporation of the Company, for adoption and approval.

7.   It is the Secretary's duty to send invitation letters to auditors, solicitors or other officers of the company whose presence is necessary.

8.   In case of listed companies, the Secretary has to inform the Stock Exchange regarding the Board Meeting.

9.   Arrange pads, pencils, a latest copy of the Companies Act, 2013, statutory registers and books etc.

10.   Arrange for sitting, proper lighting, refreshment/lunch etc.

11.   Arrange projector etc. for presentation of the project for which the company is formed.

At the Meeting

1.   At least half an hour before the meeting, the persons responsible for conducting the meeting should place the folders containing Agenda, notes to Agenda, draft minutes to Agenda, statement of expenses incurred/to be incurred, Business Plan etc. for ready reference of all directors to enable them to deliberate and discuss on each item of the agenda in detail.

2.   The Secretary's duty to keep the Attendance Register ready and obtain signatures of the directors present.

3.   Before holding the meeting accord a word of welcome to the directors.

175

4. If quorum, as required under Section 174, is present, the meeting should be called to order and names of the directors who sought leave of absence from attending the meeting should be given out. The Quorum of a company shall be one third of the total strength of the Board or two directors whichever is higher. The participation of directors by video conferencing or by other means should also be complied with for the purpose of quorum.

5. The directors who are present at the meeting may elect one of them as the Chairman of the meeting and request him to take the Chair.

6. The secretary should read the notice and explain the agenda before handing over the proceedings to the Chairman.

7. In general the secretary should help the chairman in the conduct by rendering whatever help is needed by him. He should keep in readiness all documents which are required for the smooth conduct of the meeting.

8. If any director wants to place any other item for the discussion at the meeting, then such item may be taken up with the permission of the Chairman.

9. Every director shall disclose his concern or interest in any company or companies or bodies corporate, firms or other association of individuals, by giving notice in writing in form MBP1

10.   The secretary should present the minutes of the previous meeting and get them confirmed.

11.   He should also take notes of the meeting in progress.

12.   The directors usually decide the date, time and place of the next Board meeting, the Secretary should help them in taking this decision.

After the Meeting

1.   After the meeting is over, the secretary should prepare draft minutes of the meeting, get it reviewed by the chairman of the Meeting and/or the Managing Director of the company.

2.   Thereafter a copy of the draft minutes of the meeting should be sent to each of the directors for information and comments.

3.   After seeking the comments and approval of the directors the draft minutes should be collected. Thereafter in consultation with the Chairman/Managing Director the secretary should finalise the minutes and enter them into the Minutes Book. All pages should be consecutively numbered.

4.   Such final minutes may be signed and dated by the Chairman of the meeting or by the Chairman of the succeeding

meeting. All pages of the minutes are to be initialled and the last page of the minutes is to be signed and dated by the Chairman.

5.   The minutes should be signed within 30 days of the meeting.

6.   In case of listed companies it is necessary to inform the stock exchange in specified situation as per the listing agreement under clause 49. The secretary should ensure that the necessary correspondence with the stock exchange is carried out.

7.   The Secretary should also ensure that the various resolutions at the meeting are carried out.

Specimen formats

NOTICE FOR BOARD MEETING

NOTICE OF BOARD MEETING1 Mr................................

Director,

New Delhi

Dear Sir,

A meeting of the Board of Directors of the Company will be held on............................ (day of the week), the...............................
(date)............................... (month) .... (year)

at............................. (a.m./p.m.) at the Registered Office of the Company.

The Agenda of the business to be transacted at the meeting is enclosed/will follow.

You are requested to make it convenient to attend the Meeting.

Yours faithfully,

(Signature)

(Name) (Designation)

AGENDA OF THE FIRST MEETING OF THE BOARD OF DIRECTORS OF .... COMPANY LIMITED, TO BE HELD ON......................... (DAY),..................... (DATE, MONTH AND YEAR) AT..................... (TIME) AT..................... (VENUE)

1.   To elect the Chairman of the Meeting.

2.   To take note of the Certificate of Incorporation of the company, issued by the Registrar of Companies.

3.   To take note of the Memorandum and Articles of Association of the company, as registered.

4.   To take note of the situation of the Registered Office of the company.

5.   To confirm/note the appointment of the first Directors of the company.

6.   To read and record the notices of disclosure of interest given by the Directors.

7.   To consider the appointment of the Chairman of the Board.

8.   To fix the financial year of the company.

9.   To consider the appointment of the first Auditors.

10.   To adopt the Common Seal of the company.

11.   To appoint Bankers and to open bank accounts of the company.

12.   To authorize printing of share certificates.

13.   To authorize the issue of share certificates to the subscribers to the Memorandum and Articles of Association of the company.

14.   To approve preliminary expenses and preliminary contracts.

15.   To consider the appointment of the Managing Director/Whole-time Director/Manager and Secretary, if applicable and other senior officers.

MINUTES OF THE FIRST BOARD MEETING OF..........................., BOARD MEETING NO 1/2014 HELD ON.......................... (DAY),.......................... (DATE, MONTH AND YEAR), AT.......................... (TIME), AT.......................... (VENUE)

Present:

1..........................

2..........................

3..........................

4..........................

In attendance:

....

Company Secretary

1.   Chairman of the Meeting Mr .... was unanimously elected the Chairman of the Meeting.

2.   Incorporation of the company

The Board was informed that the company had been incorporated on....... and the Directors noted the Certificate of

Incorporation vide CIN., dated .... issued by the Registrar of Companies,.................

The Board also took note of the filing of Forms INC-1, 11, 21 and 22 with the Registrar of Companies.

3.   Memorandum and Articles of Association

A printed copy of the Memorandum and Articles of Association of the company as registered with the Registrar of Companies was placed before the Meeting and noted by the Board.

4.   Registered Office

The Board noted that the Registered Office of the company will be at................., the intimation of which had already been given to the Registrar of Companies.

5.   First Directors

The   Board   noted   that   Mr. ....,   Mr.......................   and Mr........................... were named as the first Directors of the Company in the Articles of Association of the company.

6.   General notices of disclosure of interest

General notices of interest under Section 184(1) of the Companies Act 2013, received from Mr. ....,Mr. .... and Mr....................., Directors of the

Company, on ………………, were placed on the table and the contents thereof were read and noted by the Board.

7.   Chairman and Vice-Chairman of the Board

The Board decided to appoint a Chairman of the Board, who would be the Chairman for all Meetings of the Board as also for General Meetings of the Company and, accordingly, the following Resolution was unanimously passed:

"RESOLVED THAT, until otherwise decided by the Board, Mr……........................ be and is hereby elected Chairman of the Board of Directors and also for all General Meetings of the Company;"

"RESOLVED FURTHER THAT, until otherwise decided by the Board, Mr. ……. be and is hereby elected Vice-Chairman of the Board of Directors of the company".

8.   Appointment of Auditors

The   Chairman   stated   that   Messrs   …….......... Chartered Accountants, ……..............…..........., had been approached for their consent to their appointment as the auditors of the company.   A   letter   received   from   Messrs…………......,……. conveying their consent was placed before the Directors and the Board unanimously passed the following Resolution :

"RESOLVED THAT Messrs ……………..., Chartered Accountants,……………......,be and are hereby appointed pursuant to Section 139(6) of the Companies Act, 2013, Auditors of the Company to hold office from the date of this meeting till the conclusion of the first Annual General Meeting of the company".

9. Common Seal

The Chairman produced at the Meeting a Seal bearing the company's name, to be the Common Seal of the company, and the following Resolution was unanimously passed :

"RESOLVED THAT the Common Seal of the company, the impression of which appears in the margin against this Resolution, be and is hereby adopted as the Common Seal of the company".

10. Appointment of Company Secretary

The Chairman informed the Board that Mr. …………., who holds the prescribed qualification for appointment as Company Secretary and who is competent to hold the position of secretary of the company should be considered for appointment as Company Secretary. The Board agreed and the following Resolution was unanimously passed :

"RESOLVED THAT Mr………….., aged……., holding

184

the prescribed qualification be and is hereby appointed as Secretary of the company, on the terms specified in the draft agreement/appointment letter, placed on the table duly initialled by the Chairman for the purpose of identification.

"RESOLVED FURTHER THAT the Company Secretary do perform the duties which may be performed by a secretary under Section 205 of the Companies Act, 2013, and any other duties assigned to him by the Board or the Chief Executive and do report to the Chief Executive of the company".

11.   Appointment of bankers

The Chairman informed the Board that a current account in the name of the company be opened in...Bank. The Board agreed and the following Resolution was passed unanimously :

"RESOLVED THAT a current account be opened in the name of .... Limited with the .... Bank, ..., and that the Bank be instructed to honour all cheques, bills of exchange,promissory notes or other orders which may be drawn by/accepted/made on behalf of the company and to act on any instructions so given relating to the account whether the same be overdrawn or not or relating to the transactions of the company and that any two of the following directors/officers of the company,jointly, namely :

(a) Mr...Director

(b) Mr...Director

(c) Mr...General Manager (Finance)

(d) Mr...Company Secretary

be and are hereby authorised to sign on behalf of the company cheques or any other instruments/ documents drawn on or in relation to the said account and the signatures shall be sufficient authority and shall bind the Company in all transactions between the Bank and the company".

12.   Printing of Share Certificates

The Chairman informed the Board that it would be necessary to print share certificates for allotment of shares to the subscribers to the Memorandum of Association as well as for any further issue of capital. A format of the share certificate was placed on the table and the Board passed the following

Resolution :

"RESOLVED THAT equity share certificates of the company be printed, in the format placed before the Meeting and initialled by the Chairman for the purpose of identification, and that the certificates bear serial

Nos. 1 to 1,00,000.

186

"RESOLVED FURTHER THAT the stock of blank share certificates be kept in safe custody with Mr. ....".

13.   Issue of Share certificates to the subscribers

The Chairman informed the Board that Mr. ...., Mr..................................... and Mr. ....…….., who are subscribers to the Memorandum of Association of the Company, had each agreed to take and have taken 10 (ten) equity shares in the company. He further informed the Board that, pursuant to Section 56(4) of the Companies Act, 2013, the names of the said subscribers to the Memorandum of Association have been entered as the members in the register of members and that equity share certificates be issued to them. The following Resolution was passed unanimously:

"RESOLVED THAT Mr. ....………, Mr. ….............................……… and Mr....................., the subscribers to the Memorandum of Association of the company who had agreed to take and have taken 10 (ten) equity shares each, of the company, be issued equity share certificates under the Common Seal of the company and that Mr. ….............................……… and Mr. ……....................…….,

Directors   of   the   company,   and   Mr. ……………......................……, Company Secretary, shall sign the said certificates".

14.   Approval of Statement of Preliminary Expenses incurred

The Chairman placed before the Meeting a statement of expenses incurred in connection with the formation of the company. The Board approved and passed the following Resolution :

"RESOLVED THAT preliminary expenses of `..........incurred/contracted be and are hereby approved and confirmed as per the statement submitted by the Chairman."

FURTHER THAT the preliminary expenses of ` .... incurred by Mr.......*"RESOLVED., Director of the Company, in the matter of incorporation of the Company, be and are hereby approved and the same be reimbursed to the said Mr. ...., Director, out of the funds of the company".

15.   Next Meeting

It was decided to hold the next Board Meeting at .... a.m./p.m. on .... (Day),..............(Date,Month and Year) and................ (Venue).

16.   Termination of the Meeting

The Meeting ended with a vote of thanks to the chair.

....

Chairman

Entered on

Date......…....……..

AGENDA OF A SUBSEQUENT MEETING OF THE BOARD OF DIRECTORS AGENDA FOR THE.......................... MEETING OF THE BOARD OF DIRECTORS OF.......................... COMPANY LTD., TO BEHELD ON.......................... (DAY),.......................... (DATE, MONTH AND YEAR), AT..........................(TIME), AT.......................... (VENUE)

    1.   Attendance and Minutes

        1.1   To elect a Chairman of the Meeting (in case there is no permanent Chairman);

        1.2   To grant requests from directors for leave of absence, if any. ;

        1.3   To note the minutes of the previous Meeting;

        1.4   To note resolutions passed by circulation;

        1.5   To note minutes of meetings of Committee(s);

1.6   To note certificate of compliance.

2.   Directors (including, where applicable, Alternate Directors)

2.1   To read and take note of the disclosure of interests;

2.2   To read and take note of the disclosure of shareholdings;

2.3   To sign the register of contracts;

2.4   To give consent to a contract in which a Director has an interest;

2.5   To consider appointment(s) and fixation of remuneration(s) of managerial personnel;

2.6   To consider and to give consent for the appointment of a Managing Director/Manger who is already a Managing Director/Manager of another company;

2.7   To take note of nomination of Director(s) made by financial institution(s)/BIFR/Central Government/ bank(s);

2.8   To appoint additional Directors(s);

2.9   To appoint a Director to fill the casual vacancy of a Director;

2.10   To accept/take note of resignation(s) of Director(s)/withdrawal of nominee Director(s);

2.11   To consider loans to Directors;

2.12   To consider payment of commission to Non-Executive Directors;

2.13   To constitute Committees of the Board;

2.14   To delegate powers to Managing/Whole-time Directors.

3.   Shares

3.1   To authorise printing of new share certificates;

3.2   To approve requests for transfer/transmission/transposition of shares;

3.3   To authorize issue of duplicate share certificates;

3.4   To authorise issue of share certificates without surrender of letters of allotment;

3.5   To refuse to register transfer of shares;

3.6   To consider the position of dematerialized and rematerialized shares and the beneficial owners.

4.   Share Capital

4.1   To make allotment of shares;

4.2   To make calls on shares;

4.3   To forfeit shares;

4.4   To issue bonus shares;

4.5   To issue "rights" shares;

4.6   To make fresh issue of share capital;

4.7   To authorise buy-back of shares.

5.   Debentures, Loans and Public Deposits

5.1   To consider matters relating to issue of debentures including appointment of Debenture Trustees;

5.2   To borrow money otherwise than on debentures and by way of Commercial Paper, Certificate of Deposit,etc.;

5.3   To approve the text of the advertisement for acceptance of fixed deposits and to sign the same.

6.   Long term loans from financial institutions/banks

192

6.1 To authorise making applications/availing long term loans from financial institutions/banks and to authorise officers to accept modifications, approve the terms and conditions of loans, execute loan and other agreements and to affix the Common Seal of the company on documents;

6.2 To accept terms contained in the letter of intent of financial institutions/banks;

6.3 To approve draft loan agreements and other documents, as finalised;

6.4 To authorise execution of hypothecation agreements and to create charges on the company's assets;

6.5 To note the statement of total borrowings/indebtedness of the company. In case of availing of loans/financial assistance from banks/financial institutions, the draft resolutions are generally provided by the banks/ financial institutions, which may be modified as appropriate and circulated to the Directors along with the item of the Agenda.

7. Banking Facilities

7.1 To open/operate/close bank accounts;

7.2 To delegate the authority to avail bank loans;

7.3 To renew/enhance banking facilities;

7.4   To open special/separate banks accounts for dividend, deposits and unpaid amounts thereof.

8.   Investments, Loans and Guarantees

8.1   To consider investment in shares of subsidiary companies;

8.2   To consider inter-corporate investments in shares/debentures;

8.3   To consider other investments;

8.4   To consider placing inter-corporate deposits;

8.5   To consider giving guarantees for loans to other bodies corporate or security in connection with such loans.

9.   Review of Operations

9.1   To review operations;

9.2   To consider periodic performance report of the company;

9.3   To consider payment of interim dividend.

10.   Projects

10.1   To note the progress of implementation of modernization/new project(s) in hand;

10.2   To consider expansion/diversification.

11.   Capital Expenditure

11.1   To sanction capital expenditure for purchasing/replacing machinery and other fixed assets;

11.2   To approve sale of old machinery/other fixed assets of the company.

12.   Revenue Expenditure

12.1   To approve donations;

12.2   To sanction grants to public welfare institutions;

12.3   To sanction staff welfare grants and other revenue expenditure;

12.4   To approve writing off bad debts.

13.   Auditors, etc.

13.1   To appoint an auditor to fill a casual vacancy in the office of the auditor;

13.2   To appoint a cost auditor;

13.3   To appoint a Practicing Company Secretary.

14.   Personnel

14.1   To appoint, accept the resignation of, promote or to transfer any senior officer of the company;

14.2   To approve/amend rules relating to employment/employee welfare schemes, and provident fund/superannuation/gratuity schemes of the company;

14.3   To sanction loan limits for officers and staff for personal exigencies or for purchase of a vehicle, land,house, etc.;

14.4 To formulate personnel policies.

15.   Legal Matters

15.1   To note and to give directions on significant matters;

15.2   To consider amendment to memorandum/articles of association;

15.3   To approve agreements.

16.   Restructuring

16.1   To approve merger/demerger/amalgamation;

16.2   To consider formation of joint ventures;

16.3   To consider subsidiarisation/desubsidiarisation of other companies.

17. Delegation of Authority

17.1   To nominate occupier/factory manager under Factories Act; an owner under Mines Act;

17.2   To delegate powers to representatives to attend general meetings of companies in which the company holds shares;

17.3   To delegate powers to approve transfers, transmission, issue of duplicate share certificates/allotment letters, etc.;

17.4   To delegate authority with regard to signing of contracts, deeds and other documents; execution of indemnities, guarantees and counter guarantees; filing, withdrawing or compromising legal suits;

17.5   To delegate authority with regard to registration, filing of statutory returns, declarations, etc. under company law, central excise, sales tax, customs and other laws;

17.6   To delegate powers relating to appointments, confirmations, discharge, dismissal, acceptance of resignations, granting of increments and promotions, taking disciplinary actions, sanctioning of leave, travel bills and welfare expenses, etc.;

17.7   To delegate powers to grant advances to contractors, suppliers, agents, etc.;

17.8 To delegate powers relating to purchase/construction and sale of stores, spare parts, raw materials, fuel and packing materials; fixed assets; shares or debentures of companies; government securities; and to fix limits upto which executives can authorise or sanction payments; operating of bank accounts; etc.;

17.9 To delegate powers to engage consultants, retainers, contractors, etc.;

17.10 To delegate powers to provide financial assistance to employees, etc. for personal exigencies or for purchase of a vehicle, house, etc.;

17.11 To delegate powers to allow rebates/discounts on sales; to incur expenditure on advertisements, to settle claims, to sanction donations; etc.

18. Annual Accounts

18.1 To consider approval of annual accounts – after approval thereof by the Audit Committee, if any;

18.2 To approve appropriation of profits and transfers to reserves;

18.3 To consider recommending dividends to shareholders;

18.4 To take note of the Auditors' report;

19. Annual General Meeting

19.1 To approve the Directors' report;

19.2 To ascertain the Directors retiring by rotation;

19.3 To convene annual/extraordinary general meeting;

19.4 To close the register of members;

19.5 To consider matters requiring shareholders' approval;

19.6 To approve the Notice of the General Meeting.

20. Miscellaneous matters

20.1 To consider matters arising out of the Minutes of the previous Meeting;

20.2 To fix the date and venue of the next Meeting;

20.3 Any other matter with the permission of the Chair.

Secretarial Standard on Board Meetings (SS-1)

The following are the features of the Secretarial Standard-1 (SS-1) on "Meetings of the Board of Directors", issued by the Council of the Institute of Company Secretaries of India and approved by the Central Government. Adherence by a company to this Secretarial Standard is mandatory, as per the provisions of the Companies Act, 2013.

INTRODUCTION

This Standard prescribes a set of principles for convening and conducting Meetings of the Board of Directors and matters related thereto.

SCOPE

This Standard is applicable to the Meetings of Board of Directors of all companies incorporated under the Act except One Person Company (OPC) in which there is only one Director on its Board. The principles enunciated in this Standard for Meetings of the Board of Directors are also applicable to Meetings of Committee (s) of the Board, unless otherwise stated herein or stipulated by any other applicable Guidelines, Rules or Regulations.

This Standard is in conformity with the provisions of the Act. However, if, due to subsequent changes in the Act, a particular

Standard or any part thereof becomes inconsistent with the Act, the provisions of the Act shall prevail.

Following are the features of the Secretarial Standard on Board Meetings (SS-1).

Authority to summon meeting

☐ Any Director of a company may, at any time, summon a Meeting of the Board, and the Company Secretary or where there is no Company Secretary, any person authorised by the Board in this behalf, on the requisition of a Director, shall convene a Meeting of the Board, in consultation with the Chairman or in his absence, the Managing Director or in his absence, the Whole-time Director, where there is any, unless otherwise provided in the Articles.

☐ The Chairman may, unless dissented to or objected by the majority of Directors present at a Meeting at which a Quorum is present, adjourn the Meeting for any reason, at any stage of the Meeting.

Notice.

☐ Notice in writing of every Meeting shall be given to every Director by hand or by speed post or by registered post or by courier or by facsimile or by e-mail or by any other electronic means.Notice shall be issued by the Company Secretary or where there is no Company Secretary, any Director or any other person authorised by the Board for the purpose.

☐ The Notice shall specify the serial number, day, date, time and full address of the venue of the Meeting.

☐ In case the facility of participation through Electronic Mode is being made available, the Notice shall inform the Directors about the availability of such facility, and provide them necessary information to avail such facility.

☐ The Notice of a Meeting shall be given even if Meetings are held on pre-determined dates or at pre-determined intervals.

☐ Notice convening a Meeting shall be given at least seven days before the date of the Meeting, unless the Articles prescribe a longer period.

☐ In case the company sends the Notice by speed post or by registered post or by courier, an additional two days shall be added for the service of Notice.

☐ The Agenda, setting out the business to be transacted at the Meeting, and Notes on Agenda shall be given to the Directors at least seven days before the date of the **Meeting, unless the Articles prescribe a longer period**.

☐ Each item of business requiring approval at the Meeting shall be supported by a note setting out the details of the proposal, relevant material facts that enable the Directors to understand the meaning, scope and implications of the proposal and the nature of concern or interest, if any, of any Director in the proposal, which the Director had earlier disclosed.

☐ Each item of business to be taken up at the Meeting shall be serially numbered. Numbering shall be in a manner which would enable ease of reference or cross-reference.

☐ Any item not included in the Agenda may be taken up for consideration with the permission of the Chairman and with the consent of a majority of the Directors present in the Meeting, which shall include at least one Independent Director, if any.

☐ To transact urgent business, the Notice, Agenda and Notes on Agenda may be given at shorter period of time than stated above, if at least one Independent Director, if any, shall be present at such Meeting. If no Independent Director is present, decisions taken at such a Meeting shall be circulated to all the Directors and shall be final only on ratification thereof by at least one Independent Director, if any. In case the company does not have an Independent Director, the decisions shall be final only on ratification thereof by a majority of the Directors of the company, unless such decisions were approved at the Meeting itself by a majority of Directors of the company.

Frequency of meetings

☐ The Board shall meet at least once in every calendar quarter, with a maximum interval of one hundred and twenty days between any two consecutive Meetings of the Board, such that at least four Meetings are held in each Calendar Year.

☐ Committees shall meet as often as necessary subject to the minimum number and frequency stipulated by the Board or as prescribed by any law or authority.

☐ Meeting of Independent Directors. Where a company is required to appoint Independent Directors under the Act, such Independent Directors shall meet at least once in a Calendar Year.

Quorum

☐ Quorum shall be present throughout the Meeting. Quorum shall be present not only at the time of commencement of the Meeting but also while transacting business.

☐ A Director shall not be reckoned for Quorum in respect of an item in which he is interested and he shall not be present, whether physically or through Electronic Mode, during discussions and voting on such item. For this purpose, a Director shall be treated as interested in a contract or arrangement entered into or proposed to be entered into by the company:

(a) With the Director himself or his relative; or

(b) with any Body corporate, if such Director, along with other Directors holds more than two percent of the paid-up share capital of that body corporate, or he is a promoter, or manager or chief executive officer of that body corporate; or

(c)   with a firm or other entity, if such Director or his relative is a partner, owner or Member, as the case may be, of that firm or other entity.

(d)   Directors participating through Electronic Mode in a Meeting shall be counted for the purpose of Quorum, unless they are to be excluded for any items of business under the provisions of the Act or any other law.

☐   Meetings of the Board. The Quorum for a Meeting of the Board shall be one-third of the total strength of the Board, or two Directors, whichever is higher. Any fraction contained in the above one-third shall be rounded off to the next one.

☐   Where the Quorum requirement provided in the Articles is higher than one-third of the total strength, the company shall conform to such higher requirement.

☐   Where the number of Directors is reduced below the minimum fixed by the Articles, no business shall be transacted unless the number is first made up by the remaining Director(s) or through a general meeting.

☐   Meetings of Committees.The presence of all the members of any Committee constituted by the Board is necessary to form the Quorum for Meetings of such Committee unless otherwise stipulated in the Act or any other law or the Articles or by the Board. Regulations framed under any other law may contain provisions for the Quorum of a Committee and such stipulations shall be followed.

Attendance at Meetings

☐ Every company shall maintain separate attendance registers for the Meetings of the Board and Meetings of the Committee. The pages of the respective attendance registers shall be serially numbered. If an attendance register is maintained in loose-leaf form, it shall be bound periodically depending on the size and volume.

☐ The attendance register shall contain the following particulars:

(a) serial number and date of the Meeting;

(b) in case of a Committee Meeting name of the Committee;

(c) place of the Meeting; time of the Meeting;

(d) names of the Directors and signature of each Director present;

(e)   name and signature of the Company Secretary who is in attendance and also of persons attending the Meeting by invitation.

☐   Every Director, Company Secretary who is in attendance and every Invitee who attends a Meeting of the Board or Committee thereof shall sign the attendance register at that Meeting.

☐   The attendance register shall be maintained at the Registered Office of the company or such other place as may be approved by the Board.

☐   The attendance register may be taken to any place where a Meeting of the Board or Committee is held.

☐   The attendance register is open for inspection by the Directors.

☐   Entries in the attendance register shall be authenticated by the Company Secretary or where there is no Company Secretary, by the Chairman by appending his signature to each page. The attendance register shall be preserved for a period of at least eight financial years and may be destroyed thereafter with the approval of the Board.

☐   The attendance register shall be kept in the custody of the Company Secretary.

☐   Leave of absence shall be granted to a Director only when a request for such leave has been received by the Company Secretary or by the Chairman.

Chairman

☐   The Chairman of the company shall be the Chairman of the Board. If the company does not have a Chairman, the Directors may elect one of themselves to be the Chairman of the Board.

☐   The Chairman of the Board shall conduct the Meetings of the Board. If no Chairman is elected or if the Chairman is unable to attend the Meeting, the Directors present at the Meeting shall elect one of themselves to chair and conduct the Meeting, unless otherwise provided in the Articles.

☐   Meetings of Committees.A member of the Committee appointed by the Board or elected by the Committee as Chairman of the Committee, in accordance with the Act or any other law or the Articles, shall conduct the Meetings of the Committee. If no Chairman has been so elected or if the elected Chairman is unable to attend the Meeting, the Committee shall elect one of its members present to chair and conduct the Meeting of the Committee, unless otherwise provided in the Articles.

Passing of Resolution by Circulation

☐   The Act requires certain business to be approved only at Meetings of the Board. However, other business that requires urgent decisions can be approved by means of Resolutions passed by circulation. Resolutions passed by circulation are deemed to be passed at a duly convened Meeting of the Board and have equal authority.

☐ Authority. The Chairman of the Board or in his absence, the Managing Director or in his absence, the Wholetime Director and where there is none, any Director other than an Interested Director, shall decide, before the draft Resolution is circulated to all the Directors, whether the approval of the Board for a particular business shall be obtained by means of a Resolution by circulation.

☐ Where not less than one-third of the total number of Directors for the time being require the Resolution under circulation to be decided at a Meeting, the Chairman shall put the Resolution for consideration at a Meeting of the Board. Interested Directors shall not be excluded for the purpose of determining the above one-third of the total number of Directors.

☐ A Resolution proposed to be passed by circulation shall be sent in draft, together with the necessary papers, individually to all the Directors including Interested Directors on the same day.

☐ The draft of the Resolution to be passed and the necessary papers shall be circulated amongst the Directors by hand, or by speed post or by registered post or by courier, or by e-mail or by any other recognised electronic means.

☐   Each business proposed to be passed by way of Resolution by circulation shall be explained by a note setting out the details of the proposal, relevant material facts that enable the Directors to understand the meaning, scope and implications of the proposal, the nature of concern or interest, if any, of any Director in the proposal, which the Director had earlier disclosed and the draft of the Resolution proposed. The note shall also indicate how a Director shall signify assent or dissent to the Resolution proposed and the date by which the Director shall respond.

☐   The Resolution is passed when it is approved by a majority of the Directors entitled to vote on the Resolution, unless not less than one-third of the total number of Directors for the time being require the Resolution under circulation to be decided at a Meeting.

☐   The Resolution, if passed, shall be deemed to have been passed on the last date specified for signifying assent or dissent by the Directors or the date on which assent from more than two-third of the Directors has been received, whichever is earlier, and shall be effective from that date, if no other effective date is specified in such Resolution.

☐   Resolutions passed by circulation shall be noted at the next Meeting of the Board and the text thereof with dissent or abstention, if any, shall be recorded in the Minutes of such Meeting.

210

☐   Passing of Resolution by circulation shall be considered valid as if it had been passed at a duly convened Meeting of the Board.

Minutes

☐   Every company shall keep Minutes of all Board and Committee Meetings in a Minutes Book. Minutes kept in accordance with the provisions of the Act evidence the proceedings recorded therein. Minutes help in understanding the deliberations and decisions taken at the Meeting. Maintenance of Minutes. Minutes shall be recorded in books maintained for that purpose.

☐   A distinct Minutes Book shall be maintained for Meetings of the Board and each of its Committees.

☐   Minutes may be maintained in electronic form in such manner as prescribed under the Act and as may be decided by the Board. Minutes in electronic form shall be maintained with Time stamp.

☐   The pages of the Minutes Books shall be consecutively numbered. This shall be followed irrespective of a break in the Book arising out of periodical binding in case the Minutes are maintained in physical form. This shall be equally applicable for maintenance of Minutes Book in electronic form with Time stamp.

☐   Minutes shall not be pasted or attached to the Minutes Book, or tampered with in any manner.

☐ Minutes of the Board Meetings, if maintained in loose-leaf form, shall be bound periodically depending on the size and volume and coinciding with one or more financial years of the company.

☐ Minutes of the Board Meeting shall be kept at the Registered Office of the company or at such other place as may be approved by the Board.

☐ Contents of Minutes. General Contents. Minutes shall state, at the beginning the serial number and type of the Meeting, name of the company, day, date, venue and time of commencement and conclusion of the Meeting..

☐ Minutes shall record the names of the Directors present physically or through Electronic Mode, the Company Secretary who is in attendance at the Meeting and Invitees, if any, including Invitees for specific items.

☐ The names of the Directors shall be listed in alphabetical order or in any other logical manner, but in either case starting with the name of the person in the Chair.

☐ Minutes shall contain a record of all appointments made at the Meeting. Specific Contents. Minutes shall inter-alia contain:

(a) Record of election, if any, of the Chairman of the Meeting.

(b) Record of presence of Quorum.

(c)   The names of Directors who sought and were granted leave of absence.

(d)   The mode of attendance of every Director whether physically or through Electronic Mode.

(e)   In case of a Director participating through Electronic Mode, his particulars, the location from where and the Agenda items in which he participated.

(f)   The name of Company Secretary who is in attendance and Invitees, if any, for specific items and mode of their attendance if through Electronic Mode.

(g)   Noting of the Minutes of the preceding Meeting.

(h)   Noting the Minutes of the Meetings of the Committees.

(i)   The views of the Directors particularly the Independent Director, if specifically insisted upon by such Directors, provided these, in the opinion of the Chairman, are not defamatory of any person, not irrelevant or immaterial to the proceedings or not detrimental to the interests of the company.

(j)   If any Director has participated only for a part did not participate.

(k)   The fact of the dissent and the name of the Director who dissented from the Resolution or abstained from voting thereon.

(l)   Ratification by Independent Director or majority of Directors, as the case may be, in case of Meetings held at a shorter Notice and the transacting of any item other than those included in the Agenda.

(m)   The time of commencement and conclusion of the Meeting.

☐   Apart from the Resolution or the decision, Minutes shall mention the brief background of all proposals and summarise the deliberations thereof. In case of major decisions, the rationale thereof shall also be mentioned.

☐   Recording of Minutes. Minutes shall contain a fair and correct summary of the proceedings of the Meeting. The Chairman shall ensure that the proceedings of the Meeting are correctly recorded.

☐   Minutes shall be written in clear, concise and plain language. Minutes shall be written in third person and past tense. Resolutions shall however be written in present tense. Minutes need not be an exact transcript of the proceedings at the Meeting.

☐   Any document, report or notes placed before the Board and referred to in the Minutes shall be identified by initialling of such document, report or notes by the Company Secretary or the Chairman.

☐ Where any earlier Resolution (s) or decision is superseded or modified, Minutes shall contain a reference to such earlier Resolution (s) or decision.

☐ Minutes of the preceding Meeting shall be noted at a Meeting of the Board held immediately following the date of entry of such Minutes in the Minutes Book.

☐ Finalisation of Minutes. Within fifteen days from the date of the conclusion of the Meeting of the Board or the Committee, the draft Minutes thereof shall be circulated by hand or by speed post or by registered post or by courier or by e-mail or by any other recognised electronic means to all the members of the Board or the Committee for their comments.

☐ Entry in the Minutes Book. Minutes shall be entered in the Minutes Book within thirty days from the date of conclusion of the Meeting.

☐ The date of entry of the Minutes in the Minutes Book shall be recorded by the Company Secretary.

☐ Minutes, once entered in the Minutes Book, shall not be altered. Any alteration in the Minutes as entered shall be made only by way of express approval of the Board at its subsequent Meeting in which such Minutes are sought to be altered.

☐ Signing and Dating of Minutes. Minutes of the Meeting of the Board shall be signed and dated by the Chairman of the Meeting or by the Chairman of the next Meeting.

☐ The Chairman shall initial each page of the Minutes, sign the last page and append to such signature the date on which and the place where he has signed the Minutes.

☐ A copy of the signed Minutes certified by the Company Secretary or where there is no Company Secretary, by any Director authorised by the Board shall be circulated to all Directors within fifteen days after these are signed.

☐ Inspection and Extracts of Minutes. The Minutes of Meetings of the Board and any Committee thereof can be inspected by the Directors. A Director is entitled to inspect the Minutes of a Meeting held before the period of his Directorship.

☐ Extracts of the Minutes shall be given only after the Minutes have been duly entered in the minutes Book. However, certified copies of any Resolution passed at a Meeting may be issued even earlier, if the text of that Resolution had been placed at the Meeting.

☐ Preservation of Minutes and other Records. Minutes of all Meetings shall be preserved permanently in physical or in electronic form with Time stamp.

☐   Office copies of Notices, Agenda, Notes on Agenda and other related papers shall be preserved in good order in physical or in electronic form for as long as they remain current or for eight financial years, whichever is later and may be destroyed thereafter with the approval of the Board.

☐   Minutes Books shall be kept in the custody of the Company Secretary.

Disclosure

The Annual Report and Annual Return of a company shall disclose the number and dates of Meetings of the Board and Committees held during the financial year indicating the number of Meetings attended by each Director.

EFFECTIVE DATE

This Standard has come into effect from 1st July, 2015.

Chapter 5

Motions and Resolutions

Motion and Resolution

A company is an artificial person created by law. All decisions are taken by the company in its meetings. Any decision taken by the company is called resolution. So it is a legally binding decision made by company and a proposed resolution is termed as motion.

Motion

A motion is a definite proposal or an idea put before a meeting for its consideration. Such a motion may be passed without any change and modification. However in case any member feels that motion require any change they may proceeds to amendments. It is always better to be in writing as all the important matters relating to the working of company are discussed over the meeting. But for some issues like for appointment of chairman, adjournment of the meetings does not require prior notice.

Requisites of a valid motion

A motion must fulfil the following conditions:

> It is always in writing to avoid any discrepancy in future.

> It must be definite & to the point.

> A prior notice is required tobe given to all the members.

> An idea must be within the scope of the meeting.

> A motion is always proposed by one seconded by another.

> Only one motion can be moved at a time & it must be signed by a mover and when a motion is not seconded, it cannot be discussed in a meeting as it has no support.

> The wording must always be affirmative that shows an intention to do something and it must be in a proper form so that can be easily converted into a resolution. If the majority votes cast are in favour of the motion, the chairman declares, "The motion is carried".

Types of motion

Primary Motion: It means a motion related to some important function of the organisations that affects its running and working of the directors & members.

Secondary Motion: It means a motion related to some amendment of a motion. It can be an incidental motion and it does not bring business before meeting. Any amendment in primary motion can be termed as secondary motion.

Substantive motion: When any proposed amendment to a motion is being voted in a meeting & is passed then the original motion has to be altered before it is put to vote by members and such amended motion is termed as substantive motions.

Formal Motion: In a meeting, there is a possibility that members may have different opinions regarding a proposal and discussions at a meeting may be interrupted by raising various kinds of formal motions. There may be different purpose for such motions. It can be :

When incorrect procedure of meeting is followed

To raise any objection against the chairman's speech or any other matter

If any rule is being violated in a meeting

To hasten the decision by shortening discussion

When irrelevant thing are being said by any member unnecessarily & there by wasting time.

Interruptions of Debate: Interruptions to the motion may be made by means of the following formal devices:

Amendments: Amendment is one of the most common form if interruption to debate. It is a proposed modification or alteration in the words or terms of the motion which is yet to pass or consider at meeting. No prior notice is required to move an amendment. It is generally done is between the meeting i.e. when chairman invites discussion on the motion before its closure. When amendment is moved it takes priority over the original motion. If amendment is approved by majority of the members then it is incorporated in the original motion & submitted to incorporated in the original motion & submitted to the meeting for approval as a substantive motion. An amendment to a motion can be:-

➢ To replace some words by new words in motion

➢ Drop some words

➢ Change position of words etc.

Some basic rules of regarding Amendment:

An amendment should be relevant to the motion of a meeting. It should not introduce any new proposal.

It should always be done in writing to avoid any future discrepancy.

The amendment should be worded in affirmation

It should be seconded

If the amendment is carried, the chairman should incorporate the same is the main motion.

Without permission of the meeting, a motion cannot be withdrawn.

Where an amendment has been moved to an amendment, it is known as secondary amendment. It has to be discussed first if carried & should be incorporated in the amendment which is then discussed.

If the original is withdrawn, all amendments to it fall.

2. Point of order: A point of order is a tool which is used to draw a attention to a breach in rules or the breaching of established practices or contradiction of a previous decision. It can be used at anytime during a meeting including interrupting a speaker, but it must be valid, The chairman at that time must give his ruling at once and if requires allow short debate on that point. The decision taken by chairman after the discussion would be final & all members would be bound by it and discussion is resumed.

The point of order which may be raised & addressed to the chairman are the following:-

If the requisite quorum is not present.

If member notice any irregularity in a motion then he can draw an attention of the chairman to the point.

Use of offensive language by any person.

Infringement of the standing orders.

Motion not seconded by anyone.

Any obstructive activity which may affect the decent conduct of the meeting.

Difference between motion and amendment

Resolution: - The word resolution has not been defined in the companies act. It is a legally binding decision made by limited company directors or shareholders. If majority of the members vote in favour of a decision then a resolution is passed. It is a formal authorization of an action, decision &b transactions convene at a meeting which satisfies the quorum requirements. Resolutions are of four types:

- Elective resolution

- Extraordinary resolution

- Ordinary resolution

- Special resolution

The type of resolution to be passed in a meeting depends upon its particular matter. All the general business can be done by passing an ordinary resolution & for discussion on any special matter a special resolution is to be passed.

Requirements of passing a resolution

Passing the resolution at a meeting that has been properly convened & must fulfil the quorum requirement.

Then entering the resolution in the books kept by the company for that purpose within one month of the meeting being held.

The chairman must sign the meeting's minutes & that should be kept at company's registered office or at principal place of business.

If company fails to follow these requirements then the outcome of the resolution may be invalidated.

Types of resolution:

There are broadly three types of resolutions. They are:

Ordinary resolution: An ordinary resolution of a company means a resolution that is being passed by a simple majority entitled to vote therein. Votes can be cast either by show of hands or by proxy the number of votes against the matter. Thus voting for & against must both be counted & the neutral votes are to be ignored. Mostly standard business conducted at AGM's (annual general meeting) is carried out by an ordinary resolution. Under the company act 2013, ordinary resolution can also be passed by an electronic voting. An ordinary resolution can be passed for following business transactions:-

- Approval of statutory report

- Declaration of dividend

- Appointment of auditors and fixing their remuneration

- Election of directors

Removal of director before the expiry of his tenure by giving 14 days special notice to company

Appointment of another director in place of one removed etc.

Special resolution: A special resolution is a resolution of company's shareholders which requires at least 75% of the votes cast by shareholders in favour of it in order to pass. Where no special is required , an ordinary resolution may be passed by shareholders with a simple majority of more than 50% of the votes cast in the meeting.

As per Section 114 of company act 2013, a resolution shall be a special resolution when:

The intention to propose the resolution as a special resolution has been duly specified in the notice calling the general meeting.

The notice of 21 days is required under this act, has been duly given and

The votes cast in favour of the resolution, either by show of hands or by poll or electronically or by proxy are not less than 3 times the number of votes, if any cast against the resolution by members so entitled and voting.

The main objective of passing a special resolutionis to protect the minority shareholders against important decision being taken without proper considerations.

The need for a special resolution is may help good decision making , ensuring important changes are better considered & an effort made to gain wider support than a simple majority.

A special resolution is required for following purposes:

To change the company name (Section 13)

To amend the company articles of association.(Sec 14)

A reduction in company share capital (Sec 66).

Misapplication of shareholder pre-emption rights.

To have the company wound up by the court (Sec 27)

To wind up the company voluntarily (Sec 304)

To authorise payment of remuneration to directors who are not in the whole time employment of the company. (Sec 197)

A detailed statement concerning all the material facts relating to director or manager, if any shall be annexed to the notice of the meeting. A copy of every special resolution together with the copy of the detail statement shall within 30 days of the passing of the resolution be filed with the registrar who shall record the same.

Resolution requiring special notice:

The provision relating to special notice is prescribed under section 115 of company act 2013 & in rule 23 of the company rules 2014. Special notice is required in following cases:

For appointment of auditor other than retiring auditor (section 140)

For express resolution that the retiring auditors shall not be reappointed (section 140)

For removing a director before the expiry of his term (section 169)

For appointing another person as director in place of director removed (section 169)

The articles of a company may provide for additional matters in respect of which special notice is required.

Who can give such notice?

Such number of members holding not less 1% of total voting power or

Holding shares on which an aggregate sum of not less than Rs 5 lakh paid up capital on date of notice.

Time limit for special notice:

Notice shall be sent by members to the company not earlier than three months but at least 14 days before date of the meeting at which the resolution is to be moved.

While counting above time limit both the day on which notice is given and the day of meeting will be excluded.

Company duty on receipt of special notice:

After receipt of notice company shall give its members notice of the resolution at least 7 days before the meeting.

While counting the above mentioned 7 days – both the day of despatch of notice and the day of the meeting, will be excluded.

Difference between Motion and Resolution

Motion	Resolution
A motion is a formal proposal put forth before a meeting by a member for further discussion.	A motion once carried out & passed by the majority under the company act , becomes a resolution.
A motion is proposed by one member is seconded by another.	A resolution is passed & adopted by the members is binding in nature.

A motion is not required to be in writing it can be done verbally	A resolution is to be put in writing for future implementation & record purpose
It is not necessary that all motions to be carried for future & becomes resolution	All resolutions come from motions.
Motions are generally considered actions by the board of directors & not necessarily by the corporation.	Resolution adopted by the board & later approved the directors are considered a formal act of the corporation & not just a board action.
There are three types of motions :- Main motion, formal motion, & Substantive motion	Resolutions are of two types: - ordinary resolution & special resolution.
A motion can be amended anytime before voting	A resolution once passed cannot be amended.

Made in the USA
Middletown, DE
25 February 2021

34192963R00136